Druggist's Hand-book Of Medicinal Roots, Barks, Herbs, Flowers, Etc

Cornell University Library
RS 355.C51

Druggist's hand-book of medicinal roots,

3 1924 003 358 557

DRUGGIST'S
HAND-BOOK
OF
Medicinal Roots, Barks, Herbs, Flowers, Etc.

G. S. CHENEY CO.,
BOSTON, MASS.
NO. 15 UNION STREET.

CORNELL UNIVERSITY.

THE

Roswell P. Flower Library

THE GIFT OF

ROSWELL P. FLOWER

FOR THE USE OF

THE N. Y. STATE VETERINARY COLLEGE.

1897

G. S. CHENEY CO.,

FORMERLY CHENEY & MYRICK,

NO. 15 UNION STREET,

BOSTON, MASS.

IN THIS BUSINESS SINCE DECEMBER, 1844.

PRESSED

ROOTS, HERBS, BARKS AND FLOWERS.

ALSO IN BULK--CRUDE, GROUND, POWDERED OR GRADED POWDERS

HOPS

IN 1 OUNCE, 4 OUNCE AND 16 OUNCE, OR BALES-ALL GRADES AS WANTED.

PURE OIL OF

CEDAR, HEMLOCK AND SPRUCE,

IN 5 AND 10 GALLON CANS, OR BARRELS.

CANS FREE AND DELIVERED.

Hints as to time and method of collecting and curing Medicinal Roots, Barks and Herbs.

Roots and Barks of Roots, Perennials, (such as do not mature seeds the first season, but go to seed the second year,) the first year's growth only are of medicinal value, and such only should be gathered, as they become woody, and practically worthless after the first season. These are of greatest value as remedies, if collected after foliage and flowers have matured, late summer or early fall.

Large roots should be split or sliced to hasten and insure thorough drying, placed in the shade with plenty of air circulating through them.

Tree barks are best if taken off when the sap flows, or can be gathered in the winter season. From the coarser ones the outer bark is removed, the inner bark only is of medicinal value, (Cherry, Oak, Hemlock and Sassafras, being among the number), this process is called Rossing.

Herbs and leaves are best before they attain their full growth. When the flowers are in bloom, the woody stems should be rejected.

Flowers should be collected soon after opening, seeds whenever ripe. From all the above moisture should be excluded as it turns them dark.

PREFACE.

In the compilation of this HAND-BOOK, we have consulted standard authorities for correct Botanical names. For medicinal properties and uses we have taken medical works of acknowledged reputation.

Our aim has been to compile the best and most convenient Hand-book for correct and quick reference which has ever been Published, for the use of the Wholesale Druggist, the Retail Apothecary, and the Physician. With an experience of more than thirty years in the Botanic Drug trade, we have seen much of the perplexity which arises from the confusion of names given to our native plants, and we believe this little HAND-BOOK will aid others in surmounting those perplexities, and be a boon long sought for by all Dealers.

G. S. CHENEY Co.

E. M. WILLARD.
E. M. WILDER.

ABBREVIATIONS.

ABO.	ABORTIVE Capable of producing abortion.
ACI.	ACIDULOUS Substances which possess a sourish taste.
ACR.	ACRID Occasioning irritation at the top of the throat.
ADE.	ADENAGIC Acting on the glandular system.
ALE.	ALEXPHARMIC Preventing the bad effects of poisons inwardly.
ALT.	ALTERATIVE Capable of producing a salutary change in a disease.
ANO.	ANODYNE Relieving pain or causing it to cease.
ANT.	ANTHELMINTIC Destroying or expelling worms.
A-APH.	ANTI-APHRODISIAC Capable of blunting the venereal appetite.
A-BIL.	ANTI-BILIOUS Correcting the bile and bilious secretions.
A-EME.	ANTI-EMETIC A remedy for vomiting.
A-LIT.	ANTI-LITHIC Preventing the formation of calculous matter.
A-PER.	ANTI-PERIODIC Arresting morbid periodical movements.
A-PHL.	ANTI-PHLOGISTIC Opposed to inflammation.
A-SCO.	ANTI-SCORBUTIC Opposed to scurvey.
A-SEP.	ANTI-SEPTIC Opposed to putrefaction.
A-SPA.	ANTI-SPASMODIC Correcting and relieving spasms.
A-SYP.	ANTI-SYPHILITIC Acting against the venereal disease.
A-VEN.	ANTI-VENOMOUS Used against bites of venomous insects or snakes, etc.
APE.	APERIENT Gently opening the bowels.
APH.	APHRODISIAC Medicine believed capable of exciting the venereal appetite.
ARO.	AROMATIC Agreeable, spicy.
AST.	ASTRINGENT Contracting the organic textures.
BAL.	BALSAMIC Mild, healing, soothing.
BIT.	BITTER Having a tonic effect.
CAR.	CARMINATIVE Allaying pain by expelling the flatus.
CAT.	CATHARTIC Increasing the number of the alvine evacuations.

ABBREVIATIONS.

CEP.	CEPHALIC Relating to the head.
CHO.	CHOLAGOGUE Causing the flow of bile.
COR.	CORROBORANT—Strengthening and giving tone.
C-IRR.	COUNTER-IRRITANT Causing irritation in one part to relieve pain in another part.
DEM.	DEMULCENT Correcting acrid conditions in the humors.
DEO.	DEOBSTRUENT Removing obstructions.
DEP.	DEPURATIVE Purifying the blood.
DET.	DETERGENT Deterging or cleansing parts of wounds, etc
DIA.	DIAPHORETIC Promoting moderate perspiration.
DIS.	DISCUTIENT Repelling or resolving tumors.
DIU.	DIURETIC Increasing the secretion of the urine.
DRA.	DRASTIC Operating powerfully on the bowels.
EME.	EMETIC Capable of producing vomiting.
EMM.	EMMENAGOGUE Favoring the discharge of the menses.
EMO.	EMOLLIENT Relaxing and softening inflamed parts.
ERR.	ERRHINE Discharge from the nose.
ESC.	ESCULENT Eatable as food.
EXA.	EXANTHEMATOUS Relating to eruption, or skin diseases of an eruptive nature.
EXC.	EXCITANT Stimulant.
EXP.	EXPECTORANT Facilitating or provoking expectorations.
FAR.	FARINACEOUS Containing farina; mealy; employed as nutriment.
FEB.	FEBRIFUGE Abating or driving away fevers.
F-COM.	FEMALE COMPLAINTS.
GAL.	GALACTAGOGUE Favoring the secretion of milk.
HER.	HERPETIC Attacking cutaneous diseases.
HYD.	HYDRAGOGUE Capable of expelling serum.
HYP.	HYPNOTIC Promoting sleep, somniferous.
INS.	INSECTICIDE Substance that destroys insects.
LAX.	LAXATIVE Gently cathartic.
MAT.	MATURATING Favoring the maturation or ripening of tumors, boils or ulcers.
MUC.	MUCILAGINOUS Resembling gum in its character.
NAR.	NARCOTIC Having the property of stupefying.
NAU.	NAUSEANT Exciting nausea.
NEP.	NEPHRITIC Relating to the kidneys.
NER.	NERVINE Acting on the nervous system.
NUT.	NUTRITIVE Relating to nutrition.
OPT.	OPHTHALMICUM A remedy for diseases of the eye.
ORN.	ORNAMENTAL Cultivated for ornament.
PAR.	PARTURIENT Inducing or promoting labor.
PEC.	PECTORAL Relating to the breast.

ABBREVIATIONS.

PHRE.	PHRENIC	Relating to the diaphragm.
POI.	POISONOUS	Producing death if taken in improper doses.
PUN.	PUNGENT	Biting, hot, acrid; prickly to the taste.
PUR.	PURGATIVE	Operating on the bowels more powerfully than a cathartic.
REF.	REFRIGERANT	Depressing the morbid temperature of the body.
RUB.	RUBEFACIENT	Causing redness of the skin.
SAD.	SALAD	Fresh herbs eaten as condiments or as food.
SAP.	SAPONACEOUS	Soapy; making a lather with water.
SEC.	SECERNENT	Affecting the secretions.
SED.	SEDATIVE	Directly depressing to the vital forces.
SIA.	SIALOGOGUE	Provoking the secretion of saliva.
STE.	STERNUTATORY	A substance which provokes sneezing.
STI.	STIMULANT	Exciting the organic action of the system.
STO.	STOMACHIC	Giving tone to the stomach.
STY.	STYPTIC	Arresting hemorrhage.
SUD.	SUDORIFIC	Provoking sweat.
TON.	TONIC	Exciting slowly the different systems of the economy.
VER.	VERMIFUGE	Capable of expelling worms.
VES.	VESICANT	Producing blisters.
VUL.	VULNERARY	Favoring the consolidation of wounds.

G. S. CHENEY CO.,

DESCRIPTIVE CATALOGUE OF

Vegetable Medicinal Agents.

Per lb.

—— 1 ——

AARON'S BEARD. Rhus Cotinus.
    Wood. . . . . Ast.
False Fringe Tree. Smoke Plant. Smoke Tree. Wig Tree. Young Fustic.
Used in chronic diarrhœa.

—— 2 ——

ABSCESS. Polemonium Reptans.
    Root. . . . . Alt. Dia. Ast.
American Greek Valerian. Blue Bells. Jacob's Ladder. Sweat Root.
Serviceable in pleurisy, fevers and inflammatory diseases.

—— 3 ——

ACONITE. Aconitum Napellus.
    Leaves. . . . . Nar. Sed. A-phl. Nar.
    Root. . . . . " " " "
Beastsbane. Bearbane. Badgersbane. Friar's Cap. Friar's Cowl. Goatsbane. Monkshood. Mousebane. Wolfsbane. Wolf Root.
Used in scarlatina, inflammatory fever, acute rheumatism, neuralgia, etc. Must be used cautiously.

—— 4 ——

ADAM AND EVE. Aplectrum Hyemale.
    Root. . . . . . . Nar. Pec.
Useful in bronchial affections.

G. S. CHENEY CO.

Per lb.

—— 5 ——

ADAM'S APPLE. Citrus Limetta.
Lime Tree Fruit. . . . . Fra.

—— 6 ——

ADDER'S TONGUE. Erythronium Americanum.
Herb and Root. . . . Alt. Emo. Eme.
Plant. . . . . . A-sco. Emo. Eme.
Yellow Snake-leaf. Adder Leaf. Dogstooth Violet.
Used as a poultice for scrofulous sores, to cleanse and heal them.

—— 7 ——

ADONIS VERNALIS.
Plant. . . . . . Nar. Caustic Ves.
False Hellebore. Birds Eye.

—— 8 ——

AGARIC OF THE OAK. Boletus Ignarius.
" **PURGING.** (Larch Agaric.) Boletus Laricis.
" **WHITE.** (" ") " "
Plant. . . . . . Sty. Ast. Bit.

—— 9 ——

AGAVE, AMERICAN. Agave Americana.
Plant. . . . . . Diu. A-syp.
American Century Plant. American Aloe.

—— 10 ——

AGAVE, VIRGINIAN. Agave Virginica.
Root. . . . . . . Bit. Car.
False Aloe.

—— 11 ——

AGRIMONY. Agrimonia Eupatoria.
Herb. . . . . . Ton. Alt. Ast.
Cockleburr. Stickwort.
Highly recommended in bowel complaints, gravel, asthma, coughs and gonorrhœa.

—— 12 ——

AGRIMONY, HEMP. Eupatorium cannabinum.
Juice . . . . . Eme. Pur. Diu. Cat.
Sweet-smelling Trefoil. Water Maudlin.

Per lb.

—— 13 ——

ALDER, BLACK. Prinos Verticillatus.
    Bark. . . . . . Ton. Alt. Ast. Ver.
    Berries. . . . . . . Cat. Ver.
Stripped Alder. Brook Alder. False Alder. Winter Berry.
Used with good effect in jaundice, diarrhœa, gangrene, dyspepsia. The berries for worms in children.

—— 14 ——

ALDER, RED. Alnus Rubra.
    Bark. . . . . . . Alt. Eme. Ast.
    Tags. . . . . . . " " "
Tag Alder. Smooth Alder. Swamp Alder.
Valuable in scrofula, syphilis, and diseases of the skin.

—— 15 ——

ALDER, TAG. Alnus Serratula.
    Bark. . . . . . . Alt. Eme. Ast.
American Alder. Common Alder.

—— 16 ——

ALDER, WHITE. Clethra Alnifolia.
    Leaves and Flowers . . . . Dia. Exc.
Sweet Pepper Bush.
Used in fevers, coughs, and lung affections.

—— 17 ——

ALKANET. Anchusa Tinctoria.
    Root. . . . . Ast.
Dyers' Alkanet. Orcanette.
Used to color oils, ointments and tinctures.

—— 18 ——

ANGELICA. Angelica Atropurpurea.
    Root. . . . . Aro. Sti. Car. Diu.
    Leaves . . . .
    Seed. . . . .
Bellyache Root. Purple Angelica. Masterwort. Archangel.
High Angelica. American Angelica. Dead Nettle.
Used in flatulent colic, heart-burn and debility.

Per lb.

—— 19 ——

ANGUSTURA. Galipea Officinalis.
  Bark. . . . . Eme. Cat. Ton. Feb.
Angostura.
  Used in bilious diarrhœa and dysentery, intermittents and dropsy.

—— 20 ——

ANISE. Pimpinella Anisum.
  Seed. . . . . Sti. Car. Aro.
Common Anise.
  Valuable to remove flatulent colic of infants, allay nausea; and as a corrigent of griping or unpleasant medicines.

—— 21 ——

APPLE TREE. Pyrus Malus.
  Bark. . . . . . . Ton. Feb.
  For intermittent, remittent and bilious fevers; also for gravel.

—— 22 ——

ARBOR VITAE. Thuja Occidentalis.
  Leaves. . . . Sto. Dia. Ant. Feb. A-spa.
White Cedar.

—— 23 ——

ARECA NUT. Areca Catechu.
  Fruit. (Masticatory of the Orientals.) . Ast.
  Plant. (Yields Catechu.) . . . . "
Betel-nut Tree. Areca Palm.
  Used in some diseases of dogs, expulsion of worms.

—— 24 ——

ARNICA. Arnica Montana.
  Flowers. . . . . . Sti. Diu. Dia.
Leopardsbane. Mountain Tobacco. Wolfbane.
  Used in gout, dropsy, and rheumatism; the tincture for bruises, sprains, bites of insects, etc.

—— 25 ——

ARROW WOOD. Viburnum Dentatum.
  Bark. . . . . . . Diu. Det.
Mealy Tree.
  Used in cancerous affections.

Per lb.

—— 26 ——

ASH, BLACK. Fraxinus Sambucifolia.
    Bark. . . . . . . Ton. Ast.
  May be used where a tonic astringent influence is required; also as a wash in salt rheum.

—— 27 ——

ASH, MOUNTAIN. Sorbus Americana.
    Bark. . . . . . Ast. Ton. Det.
    Berries. . . . . . Ver. A-sco.
Round Wood.
  The bark in bilious diseases to cleanse the blood; berries for scurvy, and as a vermifuge.

—— 28 ——

ASH, PRICKLY. Xanthoxylum Fraxineum.
    Bark. . . . . . Sti. Ton. Alt. Sia.
    Berries. . . . . Sti. Car. A-spa.
Pellitory Bark, Toothache Bush. Yellow Wood. Sutterberry. Toothache Tree.
  A valuable tonic in low typhoid; used in colic, rheumatism, scrofula, etc. The berries a most valuable agent in Asiatic cholera.

—— 29 ——

ASH, SOUTH'N PRICKLY. Xanthoxylum Carolinianum.
    Bark, (more pungent than Xanthoxylum Fraxineum.)
Sea Ash.

—— 30 ——

ASH, WHITE. Fraxinus Acuminata.
    Bark. . . . . Ton. Cat.
  Beneficial in constipation, dropsy, ague cake, etc. The seeds are said to prevent obesity.

—— 31 ——

ASPARAGUS. Asparagus Officinalis.
    Root. . . . . Diu.
Sparrow Grass.
  Valuable in dropsy and enlargement of the heart.

Per lb.

—— 32 ——

AVENS. Geum Rivale.
    Root. . . . . . . Ton. Ast.
Bennet. Chocolate Root. Throat Root. Cureall. Evans Root. Water Avens. Indian Chocolate. Purple Avens. White Avens.
Valuable in hemorrhages, chronic diarrhœa, and dysentery, leucorrhœa, aphthous ulcerations.

—— 33 ——

BACKACHE BRAKE. Aspidium Filix Fœmina.
    Root. . . . . . . Ant. Ver.
Female Fern.
Used for tapeworm.

—— 34 ——

BALM, BASTARD. Melissa Fuchsii.
    Plant. . . . . . . Diu. Dia.

—— 35 ——

BALM, BEE. Monarda Didyma.
    Plant and Oil. . . . Rub. Sti. Car. Aro.
Oswego Tea. Mountain Mint. Mountain Balm. Red Balm.
The infusion used in flatulence, nausea, vomiting; and in suppression of urine, suppression of menstruation, etc.

—— 36 ——

BALM GILEAD. Populus Balsamifera or Candicans.
    Buds. . . . . Sti. Ton. Diu. A-sco.
    Bark. . . . . . . Ton. Cat.
Arabian Balsam of Gilead. Carolina Poplar. Poplar Tacamahac. Poplar Balsam.
Tincture of the buds used in affections of the chest, stomach, and kidneys; rheumatism and scurvy. Applied to frost and fresh wounds. Bark useful in gout and rheumatism.

—— 37 ——

BALM, LEMON. Melissa Officinalis.
    Herb. . . . . . Sti. Dia. A-spa.
Bee Balm. Blue Balm. Citronelle. Cureall. Dropsy Plant. Useful in low fevers, and to assist menstruation.

Per lb.

—— 38 ——
BALMONY. Chelone Glabra.
    Herb. . . . . . Ton. Cat. Ant.
Snake-head. Turtle-bloom. Turtle-head. Salt Rheum Weed. Fish-mouth. Shell-flower. Bitter Herb.
  Especially valuable in jaundice and hepatic diseases; to remove worms, and excite the digestive organs to action.

—— 39 ——
BALM, SWEET. Dracocephalum Canariense.
    Herb. . . . . Sti. Dia. A-spa.
Balm of Gilead Herb.

—— 40 ——
BARBERRY. Berberis Vulgaris.
    Bark. . . . . . . Ton. Lax.
Jaundice Berry. Pepperidge Bush.
  Employed in all cases where tonics are indicated; has proved efficacious in jaundice. The berries, as wash in canker.

—— 41 ——
BASIL, SWEET. Ocimum Basilicum.
    Herb. . . . . . . Aro. Sti.
Common Basil.
  To allay excessive vomiting.

—— 42 ——
BASSWOOD. Tilia Americana.
    Bark. . . . . . . Emo. Dis.
Bast Tree. Linden. Lime Tree.
  Used as a poultice in painful swellings.

—— 43 ——
BAYBERRY. Myrica Cerifera.
    Bark. . . . . . . Sti. Ast.
    Berries. . . . . . "
    Leaves. . . . . . Aro. Sti. "
Bayberry Tallow. Wax Myrtle. Wax Berry. Candle Berry. Myrtle. American Vegetable Tallow. Tallow Shrub.
  Valuable in jaundice, diarrhœa; dysentery, canker in the mouth, throat and bowels; and as a wash for spongy gums. Leaves in scurvy.

Per lb.

—— 44 ——
BAY, SWEET. Laurus Nobilis.
        Leaves and Fruit. . Aro. Fra. Ast. Sto. Car.
Laurel.

—— 45 ——
BEAD TREE. Melia Azedarach.
        Bark. . . . . . Nar. Ant. Pur.
Pride of India. Pride of China.
  Useful to remove worms from the bowels; as a wash or ointment for ring worm, etc.

—— 46 ——
BEAR'S FOOT. Polymnia Uvedalia.
Yellow Leaf Cup. Uvedalia.

—— 47 ——
BEECH. Fagus Ferruginea.
        Bark. . . . . Ast. Ton. A-syp.
        Leaves. . . . . " " "
  Useful in diabetes, cutaneous diseases, ulcers and dyspepsia.

—— 48 ——
BEGGARS' TICK, SWAMP. Bidens Tripartita.
        Herb and Seed. . . . . Emm. Exp.

—— 49 ——
BELLADONNA. Atropa Belladonna.
        Leaves. . . . . . Nar. Ano. Dia.
Deadly Nightshade. Dwale. Black Cherry Poison.
  Used in convulsions, neuralgia, rheumatism, mania, gout, and painful condition of the nervous system. Requires caution in its use.

—— 50 ——
BELLWORT. Uvularia Perfoliata.
        Herb. . . . Ton. Dem. Ner. Ale. Her.
        Leaves. . . . . Ton. Dem. Ner.
Mohawk Weed.
  For sore throat, inflammation; and as poultice in erysipelas and wounds.
BELLWORT. (Large-flowered). Uvularia Grandiflora.
        Plant. . . . Ton. Dem. Ner. Ale. Her.

BOTANIC DRUGGISTS.

Per lb.

—— 51 ——

BETH ROOT. Trillium Pendulum.
    Root. . . . . . Ast. Ton. A-sep.
Rattlesnake Root. Birch Root. Indian Balm. Ground Lily. Cough Root. Lambs' Quarter. Snake Bite. Pariswort. Truelove. Indian Shamrock. Trillium. Jews'harp Plant.
  Valuable in cough, asthma, hectic fever, bloody urine, and derangement of female generative organs; and to promote parturition.

—— 52 ——

BETONY. Betonica Officinalis.
    Herb. . . . . . Ner. Ton. Dis.
Wood Betony.
  For headache, hysterics, and nervousness.

—— 53 ——

BIRCH, BLACK. Betula Lenta.
    Bark. . . . . . Ast. Sti. Dia.
Cherry Birch. Mahogany Birch. Sweet Birch. Spice Birch.
  Used in diarrhœa, dysentery, cholera infantum, and to tone the bowels after exhausting discharges.

—— 54 ——

BISHOP'S LEAVES. Scrophularia Aquatica.
    Leaves.
Water Betony. Water Figwort.
  For flavoring medicines.

—— 55 ——

BISTORT. Polygonum Bistorta.
    Root. . . . . Ast.
Dragonwort. Easter Giant. Patience Dock.
  Used in diarrhœa, and where a general tonic astringent is required.

—— 56 ——

BITTER ROOT. Apocynum Androsæmifolium.
    Root. . . . Alt. Sud. Eme. Cat. Ant.
Catch Fly. Dogsbane. Flytrap. Honey Bloom. Wandering Milkweed. Western Wallflower.
  Valuable in chronic liver complaints, syphilis, scrofula, intermittent and low stage of typhoid fever.

Per lb.

―― 57 ――
BITTERSWEET, FALSE. Celastrus Scandens.
　　　　Bark of Root. . . . . Alt. Dia. Diu.
　　　　Berries. . . . . . " " "
Climbing Bittersweet. Climbing Orange Root. Climbing Staff Tree. Fever Twig. Fever Twitch. Staff-vine. Waxwork. Yellow Root.
　Used in scrofula, syphilis, leucorrhœa and obstructed menstruation.

―― 58 ――
BITTERSWEET TWIGS. Solanum Dulcamara.
　　　　Herb. . . . . . Alt. Diu. Sud. Dis.
Felonwort. Garden Nightshade. Scarlet Berry. Violet Bloom. Woody Nightshade. Wolf Grape.
　Employed in cutaneous diseases, scrofula, syphilitic diseases, jaundice, obstructed menstruation and rheumatic affections.

―― 59 ――
BLACKBERRY. Rubus Villosus.
　　　　Herb. . . . . . . Ast. Ton.
　　　　Root. . . . . . . " "
Cloud Berry Root.
　Excellent in cholera infantum, diarrhœa, dysentery and relaxed condition of intestines of children; as injection in gleet, gonorrhœa, prolapsus uteri and ani.

―― 60 ――
BLACK ROOT. Leptandra Virginica.
　　　　Root. . . . . . Ton. Cho. Lax.
Beaumont Root. Bowman's Root. Brinton Root. Culver's Physic. Culver's Root. Hini. Oxadoddy. Physic Root. Purple Leptandra. Quitel. Tall Speedwell. Whorlywort.
　As a laxative and a tonic in bilious complaints, typhoid fever and liver complaints.

―― 61 ――
BLAZING STAR. Aletris Farinosa.
　　　　Root. . . . . Bit. Ton. Sto. F-com.
Crow Corn Root. False Star Grass. Star Grass. Star Root. Unicorn. Unicorn Root. Ague Grass. Ague Root. Aloe Root. Colic Root.
　In chronic rheumatism, dropsy, colic, ague and female derangements.

BOTANIC DRUGGISTS.

Per lb.

—— 62 ——
BLOOD ROOT. Sanguinaria Canadensis.
      Root. . . . Eme. Sti. Alt. Ton. Exp.
Indian Plant. Red Puccoon.
    Valuable in typhoid, pneumonia, catarrh, scarlatina, jaundice, dyspepsia, ringworm, and in affections of the respiratory organs.

—— 63 ——
BLOODWORT. Hieracium Venosum.
      Herb. . . . . . Ton. Ast. Exp.
Hawkweed. Striped Bloodwort. Rattlesnake Weed.
    Used in scrofula, hemorrhages; said to be efficient against bites of poisonous snakes.

—— 64 ——
BLUE FLAG. Iris Versicolor.
      Root. . . . . Diu. Cat. Alt. Sia. Ver.
Flag Lily. Flower de luce. Liver Lily. Poison Flag. Snake Lily. Water Flag.
    A potent remedy in dropsy, scrofula, affections of the liver, spleen and kidneys, secondary syphilis, etc.

—— 65 ——
BOLDO. Peumus Boldus.
      Leaves. . . . . . Ton. Stim.
Used in dyspepsia, chronic catarrh of the bladder.

—— 66 ——
BONESET. Eupatorium Perfoliatum.
      Herb. . . . . . Sud. Eme. Ton.
Ague Weed. Crosswort. Feverwort. Indian Sage. Sweating Plant. Thoroughwort. Thoroughstem. Thorough Wax Tearel. Vegetable Antimony.
Excellent in colds, fevers, dyspepsia, jaundice, and general debility of the system, fever and ague.

—— 67 ——
BORAGE. Borago Officinalis.
      Herb. . . . . . . Sto. Dia.
Burrage. Bugloss.
    Used in catarrh, rheumatism, diseases of the skin, etc.

—— 68 ——
BOX. Buxus Sempervirens.
      Herb. . . . . . Sud. Alt. Ant.
Box Garden Edging.
    Esteemed in the treatment of syphilis, epilepsy and hysteria.

—— 69 ——
BOXWOOD. Cornus Florida.
Bark. . . . . . . Ton. Ast. Sti.
Flowers . . . . Emm. Sud.
Dog Tree. False Box. Florida Cornel. Indian Arrow Wood. Florida Dogwood. Virginia Dogwood.
An excellent substitute for Peruvian Bark. Valuable in jaundice and liver complaint. The flowers for deranged condition of the female generative organs.

—— 70 ——
BROOKLIME. Veronica Beccabunga.
Herb. . . . . . A-sco. Diu. Emm.
Beccabunga. Mouth Smart. Neckweed. Pimpernel Water.
Beneficial in obstructed menstruation, scurvy, fevers, skin diseases, coughs, etc.

—— 71 ——
BROOM. Cytisus Scoparius.
Herb. . . . . . Eme. Cat. Diu.
Broom Flowers. Irish Broom.
Especially beneficial in dropsy. Said never to fail in increasing the flow of urine.

—— 72 ——
BRYONY, WHITE. Bryonia Alba.
Root. . . . . . . Cat. Eme. Nar.
Tetter Berry. Wild Bryony. Wild Hops.
An active hydragogue cathartic, similar to Jalap.

—— 73 ——
BUCHU, LONG.
Leaves . . . . . Sti. Diu. Dia. Ton.
Barosma. Serratifolia. Long Buchu.

—— 74 ——
BUCHU, SHORT. Barosma Crenata.
Leaves. . . . . . Diu. Dia. Sti.
Bookoo. Bucku. Buku.
Useful in derangement of the urinary organs.

—— 75 ——
BUCKBEAN. Menyanthes Trifoliata.
Root. . . . . . . Ton. Diu. Ant.
Herb. . . . . . " " " .
Bean Trefoil. Bitter Trefoil. Bog Bean. Brook Bean. Bog Myrtle. Bitterworm. Moon Flower. Marsh Clover. Marsh Trefoil. Water Shamrock.
In scurvy, rheumatism, jaundice, dyspepsia, hepatics, worms, etc.

Per lb.

BOTANIC DRUGGISTS.

Per lb.

—— 76 ——
BUCKHORN BRAKE. Osmunda Regalis.
    Root. . . . . Ton. Muc. Dem. Sty.
Fern Brake. Flowering Brake. Hartshorn Bush. Herb Christopher. King's Fern. Male Fern. Royal Flowering Fern. Saint Christopher Herb.
  Very valuable in female weakness, cough and dysentery; said to be a certain cure for rickets, spine complaint and debility of the muscles.

—— 77 ——
BUCKTHORN. Rhamnus Catharticus.
    Bark. . . . . . . Hyd. Cat.
    Berries . . . . . Hyd. Cat. Alt.
Purging Berries. Purging Buckthorn Waythorn.
  Used in rheumatism, gout, dropsy, and eruptive diseases to clear the skin.

—— 78 ——
BUCKTHORN, EUROPEAN. Rhamnus Frangula.
    Bark. . . . . . . Bit. Eme. Pur.
    Fruit. . . . . Pur.
Black Dogwood. Alder Buckthorn. Persian Berries.

—— 79 ——
BUGLE, BITTER. Lycopus Europæus.
    Herb. . . . . Sty. Ast. Ton Bal.
Green Archangel.
  Recommended in intermittent fever, hemorrhage of lungs, bowels and stomach.

—— 80 ——
BUGLE, SWEET. Lycopus Virginicus.
    Herb. . . . . . Sed. Ton. Ast.
Carpenter's Herb. Gipsywort. Purple Archangel. Paul's Betony. Water Horehound. Bugle Weed. Water Bugle. Buglewort. Wolf Foot.
  Useful in phthisic, hemorrhage of the lungs, diabetes and chronic diarrhœa.

—— 81 ——
BURDOCK. Arctium Lappa.
    Leaves. . . . . . . Emo. Dia.
    Root. . . . . Her. A-sco. Alt.
    Seeds. . . . . . . Diu. Ton.
Burr Seed. Bardana Bardane. Clotbur. Hardock. Hareburr. Hurr-burr.
  Used in scorbutic, syphilitic, scrofulous, gout, and leprous diseases; the leaves as a cooling poultice.

	Per lb.

—— 82 ——

BURNING BUSH. Euonymus Americana.
       Bark. . . . . Ton. Lax. Alt. Diu. Exp.
       Seed. . . . . Cat.
Prickwood. Spindle Tree. Strawberry Shrub. Strawberry Bush.

—— 83 ——

BUR-SEED SPINY. Xanthium Spinosum.
       Leaves. . . . . Alt. Dep. Diu.
Used in hydrophobia.

—— 84 ——

BUTTERCUP. Ranunculus Acris
       Herb. . . . . Acr. Sti.
Acrid Crowfoot. Burrwort. Blister Weed. Bachelor's Buttons. Meadow Bloom.
  An active counter-irritant. The extract used with mustard to blister.

—— 85 ——

BUTTERNUT. Juglans Cinerea.
       Bark. . . . . Cat.
Lemon Walnut. Oil Nut. White Walnut.
  Used in habitual constipation as a gentle and agreeable cathartic, acting like rhubarb; also in intermittent and remittent fevers.

—— 86 ——

CABBAGE, SKUNK. Symplocarpus Fœtidus.
       Root. . . . . . Sti. A-spa.Exp.
Collard. Fetid Hellebore. Meadow Cabbage. Polecat Weed. Stinking Poke. Skunk Weed. Swamp Cabbage.
  Successfully used in whooping cough, asthma, hysteria, chronic rheumatism, spasms, convulsions during pregnancy and nervous irritability.

—— 87 ——

CACTUS, NIGHT-BLOOMING. Cactus Grandiflorus
       Flower and Stem. . . Sed. Diu. Cardiac.
Night-blooming Cereus.
  CACTUS. Cactus Opuntia.
       Leaves. . . . . . . Ref.
      Juice colors red.
Prickly Pear.

BOTANIC DRUGGISTS.

Per lb.

——— 88 ———

CALAMINT. Calamintha Officinalis.
    Herb. . . Aro. Sto. Cor. Diu. Feb. Emm.
Basil Thyme.

——— 89 ———

CANCER ROOT. Orobanche Virginiana.
    Root. . . . . . . Ast.
Beech Drops. Broomrape. Cancer Drops. Clapwort. Firrape.
    Beneficial in hemorrhage of the bowels, uterus, and in diarrhœa. Valuable in erysipelas. As a local application to arrest the tendency of ulcers and wounds to gangrene.

——— 90 ———

CANCER WEED. Salvia Lyrata.
    Herb. . . . . .
Lyre-leaved Sage. Meadow Sage. Wild Sage.
    The strong decoction or extract said to cure cancers and remove warts.

——— 91 ———

CANELLA. Canella Alba.
    Bark. . . . . . Aro. Sti. Ton.
Wild Cinnamon. White Cinnamon.
    Useful in enfeebled state of the stomach and bowels, also in scurvy.

——— 92 ———

CANKER LETTUCE. Pyrola Rotundifolia.
    Leaves. . . . . Ton. Ast. Diu. A-spa.
Consumption Weed. Lettuce Liverwort. Pear Leaf Wintergreen. Round-leaved Pyrola. Round-leaved Wintergreen. Shin Leaf. Wild Lettuce.

——— 93 ———

CANKER ROOT. Nabaeus Albus.
    Root. . . . . . . Ast.
    Plant. . . . . . . Bit. A-ven.
Canker Weed. Lion's Foot. Rattlesnake Root. White Lettuce.
    Used in diarrhœa and relaxed and debilitated condition of the bowels.

	Per lb.

—— 94 ——
CARAWAY. Carum Carui.
    Seed. . . . . . . Aro. Car. Ton.
Used in flatulent colic of children, and to improve the flavor of disagreeable medicines.

—— 95 ——
CARDAMOM. Elettaria Cardamomum.
    Seed. . . . . . Aro. Car. Sti.
A warm and grateful aromatic. Used in flatulence and as a corrective of other medicines.

—— 96 ——
CARDINAL, BLUE. Lobelia Syphilitica.
    Herb. . . . . . Diu. Eme. Cat.
Blue Lobelia. Highbelia.
Has been used in gonorrhœa, dropsy, diarrhœa and dysentery.

—— 97 ——
CARDINAL, RED. Lobelia Cardinalis.
    Herb. . . . . . Ant. Ner. A-spa.
Cardinal Flower. Red Lobelia.
Said to be useful in removing worms from the bowels.

—— 98 ——
CARDUS, SPOTTED. Centaurea Benedicta.
    Plant. . . . . Ton. Dia. Bit. Feb. Sto.
Bitter Thistle. Blessed Thistle. Holy Thistle.
Used as a tonic in loss of appetite, dyspepsia and intermittent fevers.

—— 99 ——
CARROT, WILD. Daucus Carota.
    Seed and Root. . . . . . Sti. Diu.
Bee's Nest Plant. Bird's Nest Root.
Used in dropsy, gravel, strangury, and as a poultice in foul and indolent ulcers.

—— 100 ——
CASCARA, AMARGA. Picramnia.
Ecxema, Syphillitic eruptions. . . . . Alt.

—— 101 ——
CASCARA, SAGRADA. Rhamnus Purshiana.
Sacred Bark. Chittam Bark. . . . Bit. Ton. Lax.
Intestinal tonic.

Per lb.

—— 102 ——

CASCARILLA. Croton Eleuteria.
    Bark. . . . . Ton. Sti.
Eleuthera Bark. Seaside Balsam. Sweet Wood Bark.
  Useful in dyspepsia, flatulence, chronic diarrhœa, general debility, and to arrest vomiting.

—— 103 ——

CASSIA. Cassia Cinnamomum.
    Bark. . . . . Aro. Sti. Ton. Car. Ast.
    Buds. . . . .   " " " " "
  Used as an adjutant to unpleasant medicines, and to allay nausea, check vomiting, relieve flatulence and diarrhœa, and in uterine hemorrhage.

—— 104 ——

CASSIA FISTULA. Cassia Fistula.
    Fruit. . . . . Lax.
  Used for habitual constipation.

—— 105 ——

CATMINT. Nepeta Cataria.
    Herb. . . . . A-spa. Dia. Car. Emm.
Catswort. Catnip. Field Balm.
  Useful in febrile, nervous and infantile diseases; also to restore the menstrual secretions.

—— 106 ——

CEDAR, RED. Juniperus Virginiana.
    Leaves. . . . . . Sti. Diu. Emm.
    Apples or Excrescences. . . . . Ant.
Cedar Apples.
  Properties analagous to Savin.

—— 107 ——

CELANDINE, GARDEN. Chelidonium Majus.
    Herb. . . Cat. Acr. Alt. Ape. Sti. Diu. Dia.
Tetterwort.
  Used in scrofula, cutaneous diseases, piles, and affections of the spleen. The juice to cure warts, ringworms and fungous growths.

—— 108 ——

CELANDINE, WILD. Impatiens Pallida.
    Herb. . . . . Ape. Diu.
Balsam Weed. Jewel Weed. Snap Weed. Quick in the-hand. Touch-me-not. Slippers. Weathercock.
  Recommended in jaundice, dropsy, liver complaint, salt rheum, and to cleanse foul ulcers.

Per lb.

—— 109 ——
CELERY. Apium Graveolens.
Seed. . . . . . . Diu. Sud.
Used in dropsy, incontinence of urine and liver complaints.

—— 110 ——
CENTAURY, AMERICAN. Sabbatia Angularis.
Herb. . . . . Ton.
Bitter Bloom. Bitter Clover. Eyebright. Red Centaury. Rose Pink. Wild Succory.
Useful in autumnal fevers, dyspepsia, worms, and to restore the menstrual secretion.

—— 111 ——
CENTAURY, GROUND. Polygala Nuttallii.
Plant. . . . . . . Ton. Alt. Diu.
Used in boils and erysipelas.

—— 112 ——
CHAMOMILE. Anthemis Nobilis.
Flowers. . . . . Ton. Aro. Sti. Eme.
Roman Chamomile.
Used in dyspepsia, weak stomach, intermittent and typhus fevers, hysteria and nervousness.

—— 113 ——
CHAMOMILE, LOW. Anthemis Nobilis.
Herb. . . . . . . Ton. Sto.
Garden Chamomile. Ground Apple.
Employed in fevers, colds, and to produce perspiration.

—— 114 ——
CHAMOMILE, GERMAN. Matricaria Chamomilla.
Flowers. . . Ton. Emm. Sto. Car. Nep. Ver.
Chamomilla.

—— 115 ——
CHECKERBERRY. Gaultheria Procumbens.
Leaves. . . . . Sti. Aro. Ast. Diu.
Box Berry. Canada Tea. Chink. Deer Berry. Ground Berry. Hillberry. Ivory Plum. Mountain Tea. Spice Berry. Partridge Berry. Red Berry Tea. Red Pollom. Spring Wintergreen. Spicy Wintergreen. Tea Berry. Wax Cluster.
Valuable in dropsy, diarrhœa and obstructions. The oil to flavor other medicines. The essence in colic of infants.

—— 116 ——

CHERRY, WILD. Prunus Virginiana.
  Cherries. . . . . Ast. Ton. A-sep.
  Bark. . . . . . " " "
Black Cherry.
 Valuable in all cases where it is desirable to give tone and strength to the system; also in fever, cough, diarrhœa, jaundice, dyspepsia, scrofula and general debility.

—— 117 ——

CHESTNUT. Castenea Americana.
  Bark and Leaves. . . . . Ast, Ton.
 Bark used in intermittent fever. An infusion of the leaves is highly praised as a remedy for the whooping cough. May be drank freely.

—— 118 ——

CHESTNUT, HORSE. Æsculus Hippocastanum.
  Fruit and Bark. . . . . . Ast. Ton.
 Said to be useful in gout and rheumatism. The powder of the nuts as a snuff in diseases of the head. The bark as a substitute for cinchona in fevers.

—— 119 ——

CHICKWEED. Stellaria Media.
  Herb. . . . . . Ref. Emo. Dem.
Adder's Mouth. Stitchwort.
 As a poultice to old and indolent ulcers; with benefit also in ophthalmia, erysipelas and cutaneous diseases.

—— 120 ——

CHICORY. Cichorium Intybus.
  Root. . . . . . . Ton. Diu. Lax.
  Herb. . . . . . . " " "
Succory. Wild Succory.
 Used in jaundice and liver complaints.

—— 121 ——

CHINA ROOT, AMERICAN. Smilax (Pseudo) China.
  Root. . . . . Dep. Alt.
 Used in cutaneous complaints, etc.

Per lb.

—— 122 ——

CHIRETTA. Agathotes Chirayta.
       Herb. . . . . Ton.
Bitter Stick. Bitter Stem. Chirayta. East Indian Balmony.
  A bitter tonic recommended in dyspepsia and debility of convalescence from fevers.

—— 123 ——

CICILY, SWEET. Osmorrhiza Longistylis.
       Root. . . . . . Aro. Sto. Car. Exp.
Anise Root. Sweet Chervil. Sicily Root.
  Useful in coughs, flatulence, and as a gentle stimulant tonic to debilitated stomachs.

—— 124 ——

CICUTA. Conium Maculata.
       Leaves. . . . . Nar. A-spa. Dis. Ano.
       Seed . . . . " " " "
American Hemlock. American Water Hemlock. Water Hemlock. Children's Bane. Beaver Poison. Death of Man. Musquash Root. Poison Hemlock. Poison Parsley. Poison Snakeweed. Spotted Cowbane. Water Parsley. Spotted Hemlock. Wild Hemlock.
  Used in chronic rheumatism, neuralgia, asthma, and excited condition of the nervous system. Use cautiously.

—— 125 ——

CLARY. Salvia Sclarea.
       Herb. . . . . . A-spa. Bal.
Clammy Sage. Clear Eye. Spotted Hemlock. Wild Clary. Wild Hemlock.
  Used in night sweats, hectic fever and flatulence.

—— 126 ——

CLEAVERS. Galium Aparine.
       Herb. . . . . . Ref. Diu.
Bedstraw. Catch Weed. Cheese Rennet Herb. Cleaverwort. Clabbergrass. Goose-grass. Goose's Hare. Milk Sweet. Poor Robin. Savoyan. Scratch Weed. Clivers.
  Valuable in suppression of urine, inflammation of kidney and bladder. As a wash to remove freckles, etc.

	Per lb.

—— 127 ——

CLOTBUR. Xanthium Strumarium.
  Root. . . . . . . Alt. Diu. Dep·
  Seed. . . . . Diu. Alt.
  Leaves. . . . . Mat.
Burr Thistle. Burr Weed. Sea Burdock.

—— 128 ——

CLOVER, RED. Trifolium Pratense.
  Blossoms. . . . . . Acr Pec.
Cleaver Grass.
 An extract of the blossoms, an excellent remedy for cancerous ulcers, corns, etc.

—— 129 ——

CLOVER, WHITE. Trifolium Repens.
  Flowers. . . . . . Det. Dep.
Used in ointment.

—— 130 ——

CLOVES. Caryophyllus Aromaticus.
  Undeveloped Flowers. . . . Aro. Sti.
 Useful to allay vomiting and stimulate the digestive functions, improve the flavor of and operation of griping medicines.

—— 131 ——

COCA LEAVES. Erythoxylon Coca.
Spadic.
  Leaves. . . . . . . Ner. Sti.
Used as tea and coffee.

—— 132 ——

COCASH. Aster Puniceus.
  Root. . . . . . . Sti. Dia.
Aster. Cold Water Root. Red Stalked Aster. Meadow Scabish. Star Flower. Swan Weed.
 The warm infusion in colds, rheumatism, nervous debility, headache and menstrual irregularities.

Per lb.

―― 133 ――

COHOSH, BLACK. Cimicifuga Racemosa.
Root. . . A-per. Nar. Ner. Dia Diu.
Bugwort. Black Snakeroot. Bugbane. Rattlesnake's Root. Rattle Snakeroot. Richweed. Squaw Root. Rattle Root.

Used for rheumatism, dropsy, epilepsy and spasmodic affections. Valuable in female complaints as a partus accelerator.

―― 134 ――

COHOSH, BLUE. Caulophyllum Thalictoroides.
Root. . . A-spa. Diu. Dia. Par. Emm. Ant.
Blue Berry. Blue Ginseng. Pappoose Root. Squaw Root. Yellow Ginseng.

A favorite remedy in chronic uterine diseases, and as a parturient has proved invaluable. Also used in rheumatism, dropsy, cramps, colic hysterics, etc.

―― 135 ――

COHOSH, RED. Actæa Rubra.
Root. . . . . . Pur. Emm.
Toad Root. Poison Berry. Red Baneberry. Red Berry. Snakeroot.

―― 136 ――

COHOSH, WHITE. Actæa Alba.
Root. . . . . . . Pur. Emm.
Baneberry. Necklace Weed. White Banberry. White Beads. White Berry Snakeroot.

A decoction useful for the itch. Also used in rheumatism, flatulence and nervous irritability.

―― 137 ――

COLCHICUM. Colchicum Autumnale.
Root. . . Acr. Nar. Sed. Cat. Diu. Eme.
Seed. . . " " " " " "
Meadow Saffron. Naked Ladies.

Used in gout, rheumatism, palpitation of the heart, gonorrhœa, enlarged prostrate, etc. Should be used cautiously.

Per lb.

—— 138 ——

COLOCYNTH. Citrullus Colocynthis.
 Fruit. . . . . Cat.
Bitter Cucumber. Bitter Apple. Bitter Gourd.
Is used as a cathartic in combination with other medicines. Should not be used alone.

—— 139 ——

COLOMBO, AMERICAN. Frasera Carolinensis.
 Root. . . . . Ton.
Indian Lettuce. Meadow Pride. Pyramid Flower. Yellow Gentian. Pyramid Plant.
An excellent tonic, and may be used in all cases where a mild remedy is required.

—— 140 ——

COLOMBO. Cocculus Palmatus.
 Root. . . . . . . Ton. Cho.
Calamba Root. Colomba Root. Columbo Root. Columbo.
Employed in dyspepsia, chronic diarrhœa and dysentery, cholera morbus and cholera infantum, and for convalescence from fevers, etc.

—— 141 ——

COLTSFOOT. Tussilago Farfara.
 Leaves. . . . . . Emo. Dem. Ton.
 Root. . . . . . " " "
Bullsfoot. British Tobacco. Butter Bur. Foles Foot. Horse Hoof.
In coughs, asthma, whooping cough and pulmonary affections, scrofula, scrofulous tumors, etc. As snuff in headache.

—— 142 ——

COMFREY. Symphytum Officinale.
 Root. . . . . Dem. Ast.
Gum Plant. Healing Herb. Knitback.
Useful in diarrhœa, dysentery, coughs, leucorrhœa and female debility. As an application to bruises, fresh wounds, sores and burns.

	Per lb.

—— 143 ——

CONSUMPTION BRAKE. Botrychium Fumaroides.
    Root. . . . . Ast.
    Leaves. . . . . . . Ast. Vul.
Rattlesnake Fern.
  Used in diarrhœa and dysentery, and to prevent mucou discharges.

—— 144 ——

COOLWORT. Mitella Nuda.
    Herb. . . . . . . Dia. Ton.
Mitrewort. Gem Fruit.
  Valuable in strangury, diabetes and all kidney complaints.

—— 145 ——

CORIANDER. Coriandrum Sativum.
    Seed. . . . . . Sto. Sti. Car.
Coliander Seeds.
  Used to flavor and correct the action of other medicines.

—— 146 ——

COSTMARY. Pyrethrum Tanacetum.
    Leaves. . . . . Sto. Cor. Cep. F-com.
    Seeds. . . . . . . Ver.
Ale Cost.

—— 147 ——

COTTON PLANT (ROOT). Gossypium Herbaceum.
    Bark of Root. . . Emm. Par. Abo.
  Said to promote uterine contractions as efficiently as Ergot and with perfect safety. The seed is used in fever and ague.

—— 148 ——

COWHAGE. Mucuna Pruriens.
Donkeys' Eyes. Florida Bean. Sea Beans. The Cowhage Plant Seed.
  Hairs of pods a mechanical anthelmintic.

Per lb.

―― 149 ――

CRAMP BARK. Viburnum Opulus.
Bark. . . . . A-spa.
High Cranberry. Squaw Bush.
Very effective in relaxing cramps and spasms in asthma, hysteria, pains incident to females during pregnancy, convulsions, etc.

―― 150 ――

CRANESBILL. Geranium Maculatum.
Root. . . . . . . Ast. Sty. Ton.
Astringent Root. Alum Root. American Kino Root. Stork's Bill. American Tormentil. Spotted Geranium. Crowfoot.
A powerful astringent used in dysentery, diarrhœa, cholera infantum, hemorrhage, canker, etc.

―― 151 ――

CRAWLEY. Corallorhiza Odontorhiza.
Root. . . . . . . Sed. Feb. Dia.
Coral Root. Dragon's Claw. Fever Root. Turkey Claw.
Invaluable in low typhoid and intermittent fever, pleurisy and night sweats.

―― 152 ――

CUBEBS. Piper Cubeba.
Berries. . . . . . Exp. Sto. Car.
Tailed Pepper. Java Pepper.
Useful in bronchitis, cough, and diseases of the urinary organs.

―― 153 ――

CUCKHOLD. Bidens Frondosa.
Herb and Seeds. . . . . Emm. Exp.
Beggars' Tick. Bur Marigold. Harvest Lice. Spanish Needles. Stick Seed.
Used in palpitation of the heart, cough and uterine derangement.

―― 154 ――

CUMMIN SEED. Cuminum Cyminum.
Fruit. . . . . . . Sti. Car.
Black and Sweet Cummin Seed.
A stimulant and carminative used in wind colic.

Per lb.

—— 155 ——
CUNDURANGO. Asclepias Mataperro.
    Root. . . . . . . Diu. Alt.
Condor Vine. Eagle Vine.

—— 156 ——
CUSSO. Brayera Anthelmintica.
    Flowers and Unripe Fruit. . . Ant. Ver.
Koosso. Cossoo. Kousso.

—— 157 ——
DAISY, WHITE. Leucanthemum Vulgare.
    Flowers. . . . Ton. Diu. A-spa. Eme.
Mandlinwort. Ox-eye Daisy. White Weed.
  Used in whooping cough, asthma, nervousness, leucorrhœa, and as a local application to wounds and cutaneous diseases

—— 158 ——
DAMIANA FLOWERS. Turnera Aphrodisiaca.
    Herb and Flowers. . . Aph. Ast. Ton. Exp.

—— 159 ——
DANDELION. Taraxacum Dens-Leonis.
    Herb. . . . . Sto. Alt. Ton. Diu.
    Root. . . . . " " " "
Lion's Tooth. Priest's Crown. Puff-ball. Swine Snout.
  Recommended in diseases of the liver, and in constipation, dropsy, diseases of the skin and uterine obstructions.

—— 160 ——
DEER TONGUE. Liatris Odoratissima.
    Leaves. . . . Aro. Per. Ton. Sti. Dia.
Vanilla Leaf.

—— 161 ——
DILL. Anethum Graveolens.
    Seed. . . . . . Car. Aro. Sto.
  Used in flatulency, colic, etc.

BOTANIC DRUGGISTS.

Per lb.

—— 162 ——
DITTANY. Cunila Mariana.
    Herb. . . . . Dia. Sti. Car. A-spa.
American Dittany. Mountain Dittany. Stone Mint. Sweet Horse Mint. Wild Basil.
Used in warm infusion for colds, headache, fevers, colic and nervous affections.

—— 163 ——
DOCK, GREAT WATER. Rumex Aquaticus.
"   **WATER.** Rumex Britannica.
    Roots. . . . . . . Ton. Ast. A-sco,

—— 164 ——
DOCK, YELLOW. Rumex Crispus.
    Root. . . . . . Det. Alt. Deo. Her.
Curled Dock. Narrow Dock.
Useful in scrofula, syphilis, leprosy, diseases of an eruptive nature; as an ointment for the itch and indolent glandular tumors; and in all cases where the blood needs purifying.

—— 165 ——
DOG ROSE. Rosa Canina.
    Seed. . . . . Aro. Ast.
Bedeguar. Hip Tree. Wild Brier.
Used in making conserve of roses.

—— 166 ——
DULSE. Rhodymenia Palmata.
    A Sea-Weed. . . . . . . Ant. Esc.
Dillisk.
Said to be useful in removing worms from the bowels.

—— 167 ——
ELDER. Sambucus Canadensis.
    Bark. . . . Cat. Deo. Diu. Sud. Her.
    Berries. . . . . . Ape. Alt.
    Flowers . . . . Alt. Sud. Her.
Common Elder. Sweet Elder.
The bark used in dropsy, erysipelas, and as an alterative in various chronic complaints. The berries in rheumatism and gouty affections. The flowers in erysipelas, fevers and constipation.

Per lb.

—— 168 ——

ELDER, DWARF. Aralia Hispida.
   Root. . . . . Diu. Alt.
Bristlestem Sarsaparilla. Hyeble. Wild Elder.
 Very valuable in dropsy, gravel, suppression of urine and other urinary disorders.

—— 169 ——

ELDER, PRICKLY. Aralia Spinosa.
   Bark. . . . . Sti. Sia. Sud. Eme. Aro.
Angelica Tree. Pigeon Tree. Spikenard Tree. Southern Prickly Ash. Shot Bush. Southern Prickly Elder.
 Valuable in cholera, rheumatism, colic, syphilis, toothache, dropsy, etc. The oil of the seed has been used in earache and deafness.

—— 170 ——

ELECAMPANE. Inula Helenium.
   Root. . . . . Dia. Diu. Exp. Ast. Sto.
Horse-heal. Scabwort.
 Much used in cough, colds, lung diseases, weakness of the digestive organs and dyspepsia; also in tetter, itch and cutaneous diseases.

—— 171 ——

ELK WOOD. Andromeda Arborea.
   Bark. . . . . , . . . Ast.
   Leaves. . . . . A-feb. Ref. Ast.
Sorrel Tree.
 Used in decoction in fevers to allay thirst and in convalescence.

—— 172 ——

ELM BARK, SLIPPERY. Ulmus Fulva.
   Bark. . . . . Emo. Diu. Dem. Exp.
   Ground. . . . . " " " "
   Flour. . . . .   " " " "
Indian Elm. Red Elm. Sweet Elm.
 Highly beneficial in dysentery, diarrhœa, inflammation of the lungs, bowels, stomach, bladder or kidneys, also as poultices.

Per lb.

—— 173 ——

ERGOT. Sclerotium Clavus and Secale Cornutum.
  Fruit. . . , ... Emm. Par.
Cockspur Rye. Smut of Rye. Spurred Rye.
  Extensively used in parturition on account of its power of promoting uterine contractions. Should be used only by advice of a physician.

—— 174 ——

ERYNGO, WATER. Eryngium Aquaticum.
  Root. . . . . . . Sti. Diu. Dia.
Button Snakeroot, Corn Snakeroot. Rattlesnake Weed.
  Used in dropsy, malignant fevers common to river districts, gonorrhœa, leucorrhœa, syphilis and scrofula.

—— 175 ——

EUPHORBIA. Euphorbia Ipecacuanha.
  Root. . . . Cat. Eme. Ton. Dia. Exp.
American Ipecac. Spurge. Wild Ipecac. White Ipecac.
  Valuable in bilious colic, dropsical affections, dyspepsia, jaundice, torpidity of the liver, etc.

—— 176 ——

FENNEL. Fœniculum Officinale.
  Seed. . . . . . Aro. Car. Sti. Sto.
  A good aromatic to expel wind from the bowels, and to flavor other medicines.

—— 177 ——

FENUGREEK. Trigonella Fœnum Græcum.
  Seed. . . . . Muc.
  Used in poultices and emetics where a thick mucilage is required.

—— 178 ——

FERN, MALE. Aspidium Filix Mas.
  Root. . . . . . . Ant. Ver.
Bear's-paw Root. Knotty Brake. Male Shield Fern.
  Sweet Brake. Shield Root.
  Valuable to expel tape worm.

G. S. CHENEY CO.

Per lb.

—— 179 ——

FERN, MEADOW. Myrica Gale.
    Leaves. . . . . Pec. Ast. Aro.
    Burrs. . . . . " " "
Bay Bush Buds. Dutch Myrtle. Fern Gale. Sweet Gale. Sweet Willow.
Used in scald head, itch and eruptive diseases, also in erysipelas.

—— 180 ——

FERN, SWEET. Comptonia Asplenifolia.
    Leaves. . . Ast. Dia. Ton. Exp. Sed. Feb.
Fern Bush. Spleenwort Fern. Spleenwort Bush. Sweet Bush. Spleen Fern. Sweet Ferry.
Useful in cholera infantum, dysentery, leucorrhœa, debility succeeding fevers, bruises, rheumatism, etc.

—— 181 ——

FEVER BUSH. Laurus Benzoin.
    Twigs. . . . . Aro. Ver. Feb. A-per.
    Fruit. . . . . . . Spicy.
Benjamin Bush. Spice Bush. Snapwood. Fever wood. Spice Fever Bush. Spice Wood. Snapweed. Wild Allspice.
Recommended in fever and ague, colds, coughs, and as an anthelmintic.

—— 182 ——

FEVERFEW. Pyrethrum Parthenium.
    Herb. . . . Ton. Car. Emm. Ver. Sti.
Featherfew. Febrifuge Plant.
The warm infusion in recent colds, flatulency, worms, irregular menstruation, hysterics, suppression of urine, etc.

—— 183 ——

FEVER ROOT. Triosteum Perfoliatum.
    Root. . . . . . . Cat. Eme. Diu.
Horse Gentian. Tinker's Weed. Wild Ipecac. Wild Coffee.
Used in fever and ague, pleurisy, dyspepsia, rheumatism.

BOTANIC DRUGGISTS.

Per lb.

—— 184 ——

FEVER TREE. Eucalyptus Globulus.
    Leaves. . . . . . . A-per. Feb.
    Tree. . . . . . Anti-malarial.
Blue Gum Tree. Fever Tree of Australia. Woolybut.

—— 185 ——

FIGWORT. Scrophularia Nodosa.
    Root. . . . . . Sti. Diu. Ano. Alt.
Knotty-rooted Figwort.
  Recommended in affections of the kidneys, liver, and enlargement of the spleen, etc.

—— 186 ——

FIR. Abies Balsamea.
    Balsam and Bark. . . . . . Sti. Ver.
Balsam of Fir. Balsam of Canada.
  Used in urinary complaints, gleet, inflammation of the bladder, catarrh, etc.

—— 187 ——

FIRE WEED. Erechthites Hieracifolius.
    Herb. . . . . Ast. Eme. Cat. Ton. Alt.
  Excellent in diseases of the mucous tissues of the lungs, stomach and bowels, summer complaint of children, piles, hemorrhage, dysentery, etc.

—— 188 ——

FIT ROOT. Monotropa Uniflora.
    Root. . . . . A-spa. Ton. Sed. Ner.
Bird's Nest. Convulsion Weed. Corpse Plant. Fit Plant. Ice Plant. Indian Pipe. Nest Root. Ova-ova.
  Valuable in convulsions of children, epilepsy, lock-jaw and spasmodic affections.

—— 189 ——

FIVEFINGER. Potentilla Canadensis.
    Leaves and Root. . . . . Ton. Ast.
Cinquefoil. Finger Leaf.
  Useful in fevers, bowel complaints, night sweats, spongy gums, sore mouth and hemorrhages.

Per lb.

―― 190 ――

FLAXSEED. Linum Usitatissimum.
Seed. . . . . . . Dem. Emo.
Linseed in infusion is employed in coughs, colds, pulmonary and urinary inflammations. As poultice for burns, boils, carbuncles and old sores.

―― 191 ――

FLEABANE. Erigeron Canadense.
Herb. . . . . . . Ton. Diu. Sty.
Butter Weed. Blood Staunch. Colt's-tail. Canada Fleabane. Horse Weed. Pride Weed. Scabious.
Efficient in diarrhœa, gravel, diabetes, scalding of urine, and in hemorrhage of bowels, uterus, and bleeding of wounds.

―― 192 ――

FLORIDA BARK. Pinckneya Pubens.
Bark. . . . . . . Ton. Feb. A-per.
Bitter Bark. Fever Tree. Georgia Bark.
Successfully used in intermittent fever, like Peruvian Bark in its action.

―― 193 ――

FOXGLOVE. Digitalis Purpurea.
Herb. . . . . . . Nar. Diu. Sed.
Dead Men's Bells. Dog's Finger. Fairy Fingers. Fairy Gloves. Finger Flower. Folks' Glove. Ladies' Glove. Purple Foxglove.
An active remedy in neuralgia, insanity, febrile diseases, acute inflammatory complaints, dropsy, palpitation of the heart, asthma, etc. Should be used only by the advice of a physician.

―― 194 ――

FRINGE TREE. Chionanthus Virginica.
Bark. . . . . Ape. Alt. Diu. Ton. Feb.
Poison Ash.

Per lb.

—— 195 ——

FROSTWORT. Helianthemum Canadense.
   Herb. . . . . . Ton. Ast. A-sco.
Frost Plant. Frost Weed. Rock Rose.
 A valuable remedy in scrofula, syphilis, cancerous affections, and as a gargle in scarlatina and canker; as a wash in ophthalmia, itch and cutaneous diseases.

—— 196 ——

FUMITORY. Fumaria Officinalis.
   Herb. . . . . . Ton. Dia. Ape.
Earth Smoke.
 Useful in jaundice, obstruction of the bowels, scurvy and in general debility of the digestive organs.

—— 197 ——

GALANGAL. Alpina Galanga.
   Root. . . . . . . Aro. Sti.
Amazon Root. Catarrh Root. Galangale. Galangall. East India Catarrh Root. Kassamah Root.
 An aromatic stimulant. Has been used as a snuff in catarrh, nervous headache, etc.

—— 198 ——

GARGET. Phytolacca Decandra.
   Berries. . . . . Eme. Nar. Cat. Alt.
   Root. . . . . " " " "
Coakum. Jalap Cancer. Pigeon Berry. Poke. Poke Weed. Red Weed. Red Ink Plant. Skoke. Virginia Poke.
 Valuable in chronic rheumatism, syphilis, scrofula, and as an ointment in itch, scald head, etc.

—— 199 ——

GARLIC. Allium Sativum.
   Bulbs. . . . . . Sti. Diu. Exp. Rub.
Clove Garlic.
 Recommended in cough, asthma, catarrh, hoarseness, promotes activity of the excretory organs. Externally as a counter-irritant in pulmonary affections.

Per lb.

—— 200 ——
GENTIAN. Gentiana Lutea.
  Root. . . . . . . Ton. Sto.
Bitterwort. Felwort.
 A powerful tonic; improves the appetite, aids digestion, and gives force to the circulation. Used in dyspepsia, jaundice, gout, scrofula and fever and ague.

—— 201 ——
GENTIAN, AMERICAN. Gentiana Catesbæi.
  Root. . . Ton. Bit. Sto. Eme. Ant. A-bil.
Blue Gentian. Blue Bells.

—— 202 ——
GINGER, AFRICAN. Zing ber Officinalis.
  " **JAMAICA.** Amomum Zingiber.
  Root. . . . Sto. Ton. Sti. Rub. Err. Sia.
Valuable in diarrhœa, dysentery, cholera, cholera morbus, habitual flatulency, dyspepsia, and to relieve pains in the bowels, stomach, etc. Also to prevent the griping of cathartic medicines.

—— 203 ——
GINSENG. Panax Quinquefolium.
  Root. . . . . . . Ton. Sti.
Dwarf Ground Nut. Fivefingers Root. Garantogen. Ninsin. Red Berry.
 Useful in loss of appetite, nervous debility, weak stomach, asthma, gravel, etc.

—— 204 ——
GOLDEN ROD. Solidago Odora,
  Herb. . . . . . Sti. Car. Dia.
Sweet-scented Golden Rod.
 Useful in flatulent colic, sickness at the stomach, convalescence from severe diarrhœa, dysentery and cholera morbus. Also in dropsy, gravel and urinary difficulties.

—— 205 ——
GOLDENSEAL. Hydrastic Canadensis.
  Root. . . . , . . Ton. Sto. A-bil.
Eye Root. Eye Balm. Ground Raspberry. Indian Plant. Jaundice Root. Orange Root. Ohio Curcuma. Yellow Puccoon. Yellow Paint Root. Yellow Root. Yellow Eye.
 Invaluable in dyspepsia, erysipelas, remittent, intermittent and typhoid fevers, torpor of the liver, ulceration of the mouth, ophthalmia, spermatorrhœa, etc.

Per lb.

—— 206 ——

GOLDTHREAD. Coptis Trifolia.
Root. . . . . . . Ton. Ast. Sto.
Canker Root. Mouth Root. Yellow Root.
Valuable as a gargle in ulceration of the mouth; used in dyspepsia, inflammation of the stomach, and with Goldenseal to destroy the appetite for intoxicating liquors.

—— 207 ——

GRAINS PARADISE. Amomum Granum Paradisi.
Seed. . . . . . . Aro. Sti.
Guinea Grains. Maleguetta Pepper. Paradise Seed.
Similar in effect to Pepper; used in veterinary practice.

—— 208 ——

GRAVEL PLANT. Epigæa Repens.
Herb. . . . . . . Diu. Ast.
Gravel Weed. Ground Laurel. Mountain Pink. Mayflower. Trailing Arbutus. Winter Pink.
A superior remedy in lithic acid gravel, and all diseases of the urinary organs. Superior to Buchu.

—— 209 ——

GRINDELIA. Grindelia Robusta.
Herb. . . . . . . Dem. Vul.
Valuable in Rhus Toxicodendron poisoning, asthma and kindred diseases.

—— 210 ——

GUAIAC WOOD. Guaiacum. Officinalis.
Lignum Vitæ. . . . Sti. Dia. Diu. Alt.
Pock Wood.
Useful in rheumatism, scrofula, syphilis, amenorrhœa, dysmenorrhœa and uterine complaints.

—— 211 ——

GUARANA. Paullinia Sorbilis.
Seed. . . . . . . Ast. Sti. Exc.
Valuable for sick headache, phthisic, paralysis, etc.

Per lb.

—— 212 ——

HAIR-CAP MOSS. Polytrichum Juniperum.
      Herb. . . . . Diu.
Bear's Bed. Ground Moss. May Queen Moss. Robin's Rye.
  A powerful diuretic; used in dropsy, gravel, and all urinary obstructions.

—— 213 ——

HARDHACK. Spiræa Tomentosa.
      Herb. . . . . Ast. Ton.
Horse Weed. Meadow Sweet. Rosey Bush. Silver Weed. Silver Leaf. Steeple Bush. White Leaf. White Cap.
  Valuable in cholera infantum, dysentery, diarrhœa, and debility of the bowels, and to improve the digestion.

—— 214 ——

HAW, BLACK. Viburnum Prunifolium.
      Bark. . . . . . . Ast. Diu. Ton.
Sloe.
  Valuable for canker, diarrhœa, dysentery, palpitation of the heart, and as a wash for sore eyes; also to arrest threatened abortion.

—— 215 ——

HEALALL. Prunella Vulgaris.
      Herb. . . . . Ast.
  Valuable in hemorrhages and for gargle in canker and sore throat.

—— 216 ——

HEARTSEASE. Polygonum Persicaria.
      Plant. . . . . Vul. A-sep.
Door Weed. Ladies' Thumb. Peachwort. Red Shanks. Spotted Knot Weed.
  Said to be useful in asthma, colds and fevers.

—— 217 ——

HELLEBORE, BLACK. Helleborus Niger.
      Root. . . . Dras. Cat. Diu. Emm. Ant.
Christmas Rose.
  In large doses a powerful poison. Used in palsy, insanity, apoplexy, dropsy, epilepsy, chlorosis, amenorrhœa.

Per lb.

—— 218 ——

HELLEBORE, STINKING. Helleborus Fœtidus.
  Leaves. . . . . Eme. Pur. Ver. Poi.
Bear's Foot. Bastard Bear's Foot. Fetid Hellebore. Stinking Black Hellebore.

—— 219 ——

HELLEBORE, WHITE. Veratrum Album.
  Root. . . . . Pol. Eme. Cat. Err. Ins.
White European Hellebore.
Useful in the itch.

—— 220 ——

HELLEBORE, WHITE AMERICAN. Veratrum Viride.
  Root. . . . . Nar. Sed. Dia. Eme Ner.
American Hellebore. Bugbane. Duckretter. Earth Gall. False Hellebore. Green Hellebore. Itch Weed. Indian Poke. Swamp Hellebore. Tickle Weed

Valuable as an arterial sedative in pneumonia, typhoid fever, itch, etc. Used only by advice of a physician. The powder or decoction useful to destroy insects on plants.

—— 221 ——

HEMLOCK. Abies Canadensis,
  Bark. . , ... Ast. Ton
  Leaves. . . . . . . Sud. Emm.
Hemlock Spruce. Weeping Spruce.
The bark used in leucorrhœa, prolapsus-uteri, diarrhœa, gangrene, etc. The oil in liniments. The gum used in plasters.

—— 222 ——

HENBANE. Hyosciamus Niger.
  Herb. . . . . . . Nar. Ner. A-spa.
Fetid Nightshade. Hog Bean. Poison Tobacco. Stinking Nightshade.
Used in gout, neuralgia, asthma, chronic rheumatism, to produce sleep and remove irregular nervous action.

Per lb.

—— 223 ——
HOLLY, AMERICAN. Ilex Opaca.
  Bark. . . . . . . Ton. Exp. Lax.
  Leaves. . . . . . " " "
Used in pleurisy, coughs, catarrh, gout, colic, jaundice and small-pox.

—— 224 ——
HOLLY, SEA. Eryngium Ovalifolium.
  Root. . . . . . . Aro. Diu. Exp.

—— 225 ——
HOLLYHOCK. Althæa Rosea.
  Flowers red and white. . . Emo. Dem. Diu.
Used in coughs and female weakness, inflammation of the bladder, retention of urine, affection of the kidneys, etc.

—— 226 ——
HONEYSUCKLE, BUSH. Diervilla Canandensis.
  Leaves and Root. . . . . Diu. Alt.
Employed for gravel, gleet, syphilis, inflammation of the bladder, scrofula, etc.

—— 227 ——
HOPS. Humulus Lupulus.
  Flowers. . Bit. Ner. Ano. Ton. Hyp. Feb. Diu.
Lupuline.
Valuable as a sedative to produce sleep and in nervousness, delirium tremens; externally as fomentation in cramps, pains, swellings, indolent ulcers, salt rheum, tumors, etc.

—— 228 ——
HOREHOUND. Marrubium Vulgare.
  Herb. . . . . . Sti. Ton. Exd. Diu.
White Horehound.
Useful in coughs, colds, chronic catarrh, asthma and pulmonary affections; the cold infusion in dyspepsia, and as a vermifuge.

—— 229 ——
HORSE RADISH. Nasturtium Armoracia.
  Leaves. . . . Sti. Diu. A-sco. Rub. Emm.
  Root. . . . " " " " "
Used with advantage in paralysis, rheumatism, dropsy and scurvy. Grated with sugar for hoarseness.

——— 230 ———

HORSE WEED. Ambrosia Trifida.
  Herb. . . . . . Sti. Ast. A-sep. Opt.
Tall Ambrosia.

——— 231 ———

HOUND'S TONGUE. Cynoglossum Officinale.
  Plant. . . . . Ast. Ano.
Canadian Bur. Tory Weed.
 Indicated in hemorrhages, dysentery, coughs, etc.

——— 232 ———

HOUSE LEEK. Sempervivum Tectorum.
  Leaves. . . . . . . Dis. Ref.
Bullock's Eye. Thunder Plant.
 The leaves steeped form a cooling application to burns, stings of insects, erysipelas and sores, ringworm, warts, etc.

——— 233 ———

HOUSE LEEK, SMALL. Sedum Acre.
  Plant. . . . Acr. Eme. Cat. Ves. Diu.
Biting Stone Crop.

——— 234 ———

HYDRANGEA. Hydrangea Arborescens.
  Root. . . . . Diu.
Seven Barks. Wild Hydrangea.
 Valuable to remove gravel and brick-dust deposits from the bladder, and to relieve excruciating pains caused thereby.

——— 235 ———

HYSSOP. Hyssopus Officinalis.
  Herb. . . . . . Sti. Aro. Car. Ton.
 Valuable in quinsy, asthma and chest diseases; the leaves applied to bruises remove pain and discoloration.

——— 236 ———

ICELAND MOSS. Cetraria Islandica.
  Moss. . . . . . Dem. Ton. Nut.
 Used in chronic catarrh, dysentery, diarrhœa, and as a tonic in dyspepsia, convalescence and exhausting diseases.

	Per lb.

—— 237 ——

INDIAN CUP. Silphium Perfoliatum.
        Plant. . . . . . Dia. Sti. Alt.
Ragged Cup. Rosin Weed.
  Used in cough and painful affections of the chest.

—— 238 ——

INDIAN HEMP, AMERICAN. Cannabis Sativa var. Indica.
        Extract. . . Ner. Ano. Sud. A-spa. A-syp.
        Seeds yield oil.
Neckweed.

—— 239 ——

INDIAN HEMP, BLACK. Apocynum Cannabinum.
        Root. . . . . . Nau. Cat. Dia.
  Used in dropsy, remittent and intermittent fevers, pneumonia, obstructions of the kidneys, liver and spleen.

—— 240 ——

INDIAN HEMP, WHITE. Asclepias Incarnata.
        Root. . . Diu. Eme. Ant. Ver. Cat.
Flesh-colored Asclepias. Rose-colored Silkweed. Swamp Milkweed. Water Nerve Root.
  Recommended in rheumatic, asthmatic, catarrhal and syphilitic affections, and as a vermifuge.

—— 241 ——

INDIAN PHYSIC. Gillenia Trifoliata.
        Root. . . . Eme. Cat. Sud. Ton.
Indian Hippo. Meadow Sweet.
  Valuable in amenorrhœa, rheumatism, dropsy, costiveness, dyspepsia, worms and intermittents.

—— 242 ——

INDIAN TURNIP. Arisæma Triphyllum.
        Root. . . . . . Acr. Exp. Dia.
Bog Onion. Cuckoo Pint. Dragon Root. Dragon Turnip. Jack-in-the-pulpit. Lords and Ladies. Meadow Turnip. Marsh Turnip. Pepper Turnip. Priest's Pintle. Swamp Turnip. Starchwort. Three-leaved Arum. Wake Robin. Wild Turnip.
  Recommended in croup, cough, asthma, bronchitis, pain in the chest, colic, low typhoid, and externally in scrofulus tumors, scald head, etc.

Per lb.

—— 243 ——

INDIGO, WILD. Baptisia Tinctoria.
    Herb and Root. . . Pur. Eme. Sti. A-sep.
Clover Broom. Horsefly Weed. Horse Fleaweed. Indigo Weed. Indigo Broom. Rattle-bush. False Wild Indigo. Yellow Indigo. Yellow Broom.
Valuable as a wash in all species of ulcer, as malignant sore mouth and throat, mercurial sore mouth, scrofulous or syphilitic ophthalmia, fetid leucorrhœa and discharges.

—— 244 ——

IRISH MOSS. Chondrus Crispus.
    Carragheen. . . . . Nut. Dem.
Pearl Moss. Salt Rock Moss.
Used in cough, colds and pulmonary affections, chronic diarrhœa, dysentery, scrofula and rickets; boiled in milk is a nutritious tonic.

—— 245 ——

IRON WOOD, Ostrya Virginica.
    Bark. . . . . . A-per. Ton. Alt.
Employed in intermittent fever, neuralgia, dyspepsia, scrofula and indigestion.

—— 246 ——

IVY, AMERICAN, Ampelopsis Quinquefolia.
    Bark. . . . . Alt. Ton. Ast. Exp.
Five Leaves. False Grapes. Virginia Creeper. Woodbine. Wild Woodvine. Woody Climber.
Used in syrups for scrofula, syphilis, dropsy, bronchitis and pulmonary complaints.

—— 247 ——

IVY, GROUND. Nepeta Glechoma.
    Herb. . . . . . Sti. Ton. Pec.
Ale Hoof. Cat's paw. Catfoot. Carrion Flower. Gillrun. Gill-over-the-ground. Haymaids. Hedgemaids. Hove. Robin-run-away. Robin-run-in-the-hedge. Tun Hoof.
Used in diseases of the lungs and kidneys, asthma, jaundice and lead colic.

Per lb.

—— 248 ——

JABORANDI. Pilocarpus Selloanus.
   Leaves. . . . . Sia.
A valuable sudorific, sialagogue and moderator of febrile action.

—— 249 ——

JACOB'S LADDER. Smilax Peduncularis.
   Herb. . . . . Diu. Emm.
Valuable in kidney diseases, stone in the bladder, falling of the womb.

—— 250 ——

JALAP. Ipomœa Jalapa.
   Root. . . . . Cat.
Much used as a purgative in dropsy and some forms of scrofula where a powerful cathartic is required.

—— 251 ——

JESSAMINE, YELLOW. Gelsemium Sempervirens.
   Root. . . . . Feb.
Carolina Jessamine. Wild Jessamine. Woodbine.
A valuable febrifuge in all fevers, except congestive; also used in nervous irritability, headache, lock-jaw, and to promote contraction of the uterus.

—— 252 ——

JOB'S TEARS. Coix Lachryma.
   Seed . . . . Diu. Ton.
Said to dissolve calculi; used also in dropsy and incontinence of urine.

—— 253 ——

JOHNSWORT. Hypericum Perforatum.
   Herb. . . . . . . Ast. Sed. Diu.
St. Johnswort.
Used in suppression of urine, chronic urinary affections, diarrhœa, dysentery, worms, jaundice and menorrhagia. In ointment for wounds, ulcers, caked breast, tumors, etc.

BOTANIC DRUGGISTS.

Per lb.

—— 254 ——
JUNIPER BERRIES. Juniperus Communis.
        Berries. . . . . . Sti. Car. Diu.
Juniper Bush.
    Efficacious in gonorrhœa, gleet, leucorrhœa, affections of the skin, scrbutic diseases, dropsy, and kidney complaints generally.

—— 255 ——
KNOT GRASS. Triticum Repens.
        Root. . . . . . . Diu. Ape.
Bird Weed. Couch Grass. Chiendent. Dog Grass. Dog Weed. Quick or Quitch Grass. Quickens. Quack Grass. Quitch. Witch Grass.
    Valuable in kidney diseases, irritation of the bladder and spasmodic affections.

—— 256 ——
KING'S CLOVER. Melilotus Officinalis.
        Herb. . . . . . . Emo. Diu.
Melilot. Sweet Clover. Sweet Lucerne.
    The leaves and flowers boiled in lard are useful in all kinds of ulcers, inflammations, burns, etc.

—— 257 ——
KOLA. Cola Acuminata.
        Nut. . . . . . . Ton. Stim. Ast.
Used in nervous troubles.

—— 258 ——
LABRADOR TEA. Ledum Latifolium.
        Herb. . . . . . . Pec. Ton.
Useful in coughs, dyspepsia, dysentery, and skin diseases.

—— 259 ——
LARKSPUR. Delphinium Consolida.
        Herb. . . . Eme. Cat. Diu. Nar.
        Seed. . . . . " " " "
Knight's Spur. Lark Heel. Lark's Claw.
    Used externally as ointment in cutaneous diseases and to destroy insects on the body, lice, etc.

—— 260 ——
LAUREL, MOUNTAIN. (Broad-leaved.) Kalmia Latifolia.
        Leaves. . Nar. Poi. Alt. Err. A-syp. Sed. Ast.
American Laurel. Big-leaved Ivy. Broad-leaved Kalmia. Calico Bush. Spoonhunt.
    Used in scrofula and cutaneous affections.

—— 261 ——

Per lb.

LAUREL, SHEEP. (Narrow-leaved.) Kalmia Angustifolia.
    Leaves.   Nar. Poi. Alt. A-syp. Sed. Ast. Err.
Lambkill. Ivy. Laurel Poison. Sheep Poison.
  Used in syphilitic diseases, scald head, cutaneous affections, hemorrhages, diarrhœa and flux.

—— 262 ——

LAVENDER. Lavandula Vera.
    Flowers. . . . . Car. Ton. Sti.
Garden Lavender.
  Valuable in flatulency, fainting and to arrest vomiting. Usually combined with other medicines.

—— 263 ——

LEATHERWOOD. Dirca Palustris.
    Bark. . . . Eme. Acr. Rub. Sud. Exp.
American Mezereon. Leather Bush. Moosewood. Rope Bark. Leaver Wood.
  A poultice of the bark will produce vesication. Used in combination with alteratives.

—— 264 ——

LETTUCE, ACRID. Lectuca Virosa.
  Juice is used in the manufacture of German Lactucarium.

—— 265 ——

LETTUCE, GARDEN. Lactuca Sativa.
    Herb. . . . . . Diu. Nar. Hyp.
    Leaves. . . . . . . Sad.
    Juice. . . . . . . Ano. Hyp.
Sleepwort. Salad.
  Used as a narcotic where Opium is objectionable.

—— 266 ——

LETTUCE, WILD. Lactuca Elongata.
    Herb. . . . Nar. Sed. Ano. Hyp. Dia.
Snakeweed. Snake Bite.
  Similar to Garden Lettuce in effect.

BOTANIC DRUGGISTS.

Per lb.

—— 267 ——
LIFE EVERLASTING. Gnaphalium Polycephalum.
Herb. . . . . Ast. Dia.
Balsam Weed. Chafe Weed. Cud Weed. Field Balsam. Golden Motherwort. Indian Posey. Poverty Weed. Sweet-scented Life Everlasting. Sweet Balsam. White Balsam.
Used for bowel complaints, coughs, colds, bleeding of the lungs, and to produce perspiration.

—— 268 ——
LIFE ROOT. Senecio Aureus and Senecio Gracilis.
Herb and Root. . . Diu. Dia. Ton. Aro.
Cough Weed. Cocash Weed. Female Regulator. False Valerian. Golden Senecio. Ragwort. Squaw Weed. Uncum. Waw Weed.
Valuable in profuse menstruation, gravel, strangury, and for the peculiar influence it has upon the female reproductive organs.

—— 269 ——
LILY OF THE VALLEY. Convallaria Majalis.
Root and Leaves. . . . . . Diu.
Used in dropsy.

—— 270 ——
LILY, WHITE. Nymphæa Odorata.
Root. . . . . . . Ast. Vul. Dis.
Flowers. . . . . . . Orn. Per.
Cow Cabbage. Pond Lily. Sweet-scented Water Lily. Toad Lily. White Pond Lily. Water Cabbage.
Useful in dysentery, diarrhœa, leucorrhœa and scrofula. Combined with Cherry Bark for bronchial affections. Externally as poultice for boils, tumors, scrofulous ulcers, etc.

—— 271 ——
LILY ROOT, YELLOW. Nuphar Advena.
Root. . . Ast. Dem. Dis. Emo. F-com.
Brandybottles. Beaver Root. Cow Lily. Yellow Pond Lily. Frog Lily. Spatter Dock.
Properties very similar to White Lily.

—— 272 ——
LINDEN FLOWERS. Tilia Europœa and Americana.
Bark and Flowers. . . . . Ast. Dem.
Basswood. Lime Tree. Locust Bloom. Tilia Flowers.
For poultice in painful swellings.

	Per lb.

—— 273 ——

LICORICE. Glycyrrhiza Glabra.
       Root. . . . .   Nut. Dem. Exp. Lax.
       Extract. . . .   "   "   "   "

Licorice. Spanish Juice. Sweet Liquorice. Sweet Wood.
  Useful in coughs, catarrh, irritation of the urinary organs, pain of the intestines in diarrhœa, and bronchial affections.

—— 274 ——

LIVERWORT. Hepatica Triloba.
       Herb. . . . . .   Muc. Ast. Pec.

Crystalwort. Kidney Liver Leaf. Liver Moss. Liver Weed. Liver Leaf. Noble Liverwort. Trefoil.
  Used in fevers, hepatic complaints, bleeding of the lungs, coughs, etc.

—— 275 ——

LOBELIA. Lobelia Inflata.
       Herb. . . . .   A-spa. Eme. Exp. Dia.
       Seed. . . . .   "   "   "   "

Asthma Weed. Bladder Podded Lobelia. Emetic Weed. Emetic Herb. Eyebright. Gag Root. Puke Weed. Vomitwort. Wild and Indian Tobacco.
  Invaluable in spasmodic asthma, croup, pneumonia catarrh, epilepsy, hysteria, cramps, and convulsions. Externally as poultice in sprains, bruises, felons, ringworm, erysipelas, and stings of insects, ivy poison, etc.

—— 276 ——

LOVAGE. Ligusticum Levisticum.
       Leaves. . . . .   Aro. Car. Dia.
       Root. . . . .   "   "   "
       Seed. . . . .   "   "   "

Lavose. Smellage. Sea Parsley.
  Combined with other drugs as a corrective and for its flavor. Sometimes used in female complaints and nervousness.

BOTANIC DRUGGISTS.

Per lb.

—— 277 ——

LUNGWORT. Pulmonaria Officinalis.
  Plant . . . . Pec. Exp. Dem.
Spotted Comfrey. Spotted Lungwort. Virginia Cowslip.
 Used in diseases of the lungs, coughs, influenza, catarrh, etc.

—— 278 ——

LUNGWORT, MAPLE. Sticta Pulmonaria.
  Plant. . . . . Bit. Ton.
Tree Lungwort.
 Used in pulmonary complaints.

—— 279 ——

MAGNOLIA. Magnolia Glauca.
  Bark. . . . . . . Aro. Ton. Dia.
Beaver Tree. Sweet Magnolia. Swamp Sassafras. White Bay.
 Useful in intermittent fever, dyspepsia, erysipelas, dysentery, leucorrhœa, and as wash in tetter, salt rheum, etc.

—— 280 ——

MAIDENHAIR. Adiantum Pedatum.
  Herb. . . . . Ref. Exp. Ton. Sud. Ast.
Rock Fern.
 Valuable in cough, asthma, hoarseness, influenza. pleurisy jaundice, febrile diseases and erysipelas.

—— 281 ——

MALLOW, LOW. Malva Rotundifolia.
  Leaves. . . . . . . Dem. Diu.
Blue Mallows. Cheeses. Dwarf Mallow.
 Used for cough, irritation of the bowels, kidneys and urinary organs, and as poultice for boils, etc.

—— 282 ——

MALLOW, MARSH. Althæa Officinalis.
  Flowers. . . . . . . Dem. Diu.
  Leaves. . . . . . . " "
  Root. . . . . " "
Mortification Root. Sweat Weed. Wymote.
 Valuable in hoarseness, catarrh, pneumonia, gonorrhœa, venal irritation, dysentery strangury, gravel and all kidney complaints; and as poultice in all painful swellings.

Per lb.

—— 283 ——
MANDRAKE. Podophyllum Peltatum.
    Root. . . . . Cat. Alt. Ant. Hyd. Sia.
American Mandrake. Duck's Foot. Ground Lemon. Hog Apple. Indian Apple. May Apple. Raccoon Berry. Wild Lemon. Wild Mandrake. Yellow Berry.
Valuable in jaundice, bilious and intermittent fever, scrofula, syphilis, liver complaint, rheumatism, and where a powerful cathartic is required.

—— 284 ——
MAN ROOT. Convolvulus Panduratus.
    Root. . . . . . . Cat.
Bindweed. Kussander. Man-in-the-ground. Mechameck. Mechoacan. Man-of-the-earth. Wild Scammony. Wild Rhubarb. Wild Jalap. Wild Potato.
Has been recommended in dropsy, strangury and calculous affections, diseases of the lungs, liver and kidneys.

—— 285 ——
MAPLE, RED. Acer Rubrum.
    Bark. . . . . . . Ton. Ant.
Swamp Maple. Whistle Wood.
Used for worms, as a gentle tonic, and as a wash for sore eyes.

—— 286 ——
MARIGOLD. Calendula Officinalis.
    Flowers. . . . . . . Sti. Dia.
Mary Bud.
Valuable in keeping out eruptions; and the tincture for cuts, bruises, sprains, wounds, etc., and to prevent gangrene is unequalled.

—— 287 ——
MARJORAM, SWEET. Origanum Marjorana.
    Herb. . . . . . Sti. Ton. Emm.
Promotes perspiration, menstruation when recently stopped, relieves eruptive diseases.

—— 288 ——
MARSH ROSEMARY. Statice Caroliniana.
    Root. . . . . . . Ast.
American Thrift. Canker Root. Ink Root. Meadow Root. Lavender Thrift. Sea Lavender.
A domestic remedy for dysentery, diarrhœa, canker, leucorrhœa, gleet, etc.

BOTANIC DRUGGISTS. 57

Per lb.

—— 289 ——
MASTERWORT. Heracleum Lanatum.
    Root. . . . . . . Sti. A-spa. Car.
    Seed. . . . . . . " " "
Cow Parsnip.
  Used in flatulency, dyspepsia, epilepsy, asthma, amenorrhœa, colic, dysmenorrhœa, palsy, apoplexy, etc.

—— 290 ——
MATICO PLANT. Artanthe Elongata.
    Leaves. . Sty. Aro. Bit. Sti. Vul. Aph. A-syp.
Pepper Elder. Soldiers' Herb.
  Recommended in bleeding at the lungs, stomach or kidneys, flour-albus, gonorrhœa, piles, dyspepsia, and to arrest hemorrhage from wounds, insect bites, etc.

—— 291 ——
MAYWEED. Anthemis Cotula.
    Herb. . . . . Ton. Eme. A-spa. Emm.
Dog Fennel. Dillydil Weed. Fieldwort. Field Weed. Maywort. Stinking Chamomile. Wild Chamomile.
  Used in colds to produce perspiration, also in sick headache, amenorrhœa and convalescence from fevers.

—— 292 ——
MEZEREON. Daphne Mezereum.
    Bark. . . . . . Sti. Alt. Diu. Nar.
Spurge Olive.
  In small doses used in syphilis, scrofula, chronic rheumatism, mercurial syphilis and diseases of the skin.

—— 293 ——
MILKWEED. Asclepias Cornuti (Syriaca).
    Root. . . . . . Ano. Emm. Diu. Alt.
Silkweed. Common Silkweed. Common Milkweed. Silky Swallowwort. Swallowwort.
  Valuable in amenorrhœa, dropsy, retention of urine, dyspepsia, asthma and scrofulous diseases.

—— 294 ——
MINT, HORSE. Monarda Punctata.
    Herb. . . . Sti. Car. Sud. Diu. A-Eme.
  Used in flatulence, nausea, vomiting, suppression of urine, and as an emmenagogue.

G. S. CHENEY CO.

Per lb.

―― 295 ――
MINT, MOUNTAIN. Pycnanthemum Montanum.
Herb. . . . . . Sti. Ton. Emm.
Used for obstructed menstruation, to produce perspiration, and in colds, fevers and eruptions.

―― 296 ――
MISTLETOE. Viscum Verticillatum.
Leaves and Twigs. . . . A-spa. Nar. Ton.
Golden-bough.
Said to be useful for pleurisy, vertigo. dysentery, chorea and epilepsy.

―― 297 ――
MOCCASIN ROOT. Cypripedium Pubescens.
Root. . . . . Ton. Sti. Dia. A-spa.
American Valerian. Ladies' Slipper. Nerve Root. Noah's Ark. Bleeding Heart. Indian Shoe. Yellow Moccasin. Pine Tulip. Monkey Flower. Slipper Root. Umbel. Yellow Ladies' Slipper. Yellow Umbel. Venus' Cup. Venus' Shoe.
Invaluable in nervousness, headache, hysterics, and all cases of nervous irritability.

―― 298 ――
MOTHERWORT. Leonurus Cardiaca.
Herb. . . . . Emm. Ner. A-spa. Lax.
Lion's Ear. Lion's Tail. Throwwort.
Valuable in female complaints, nervousness, colds, delirium, wakefulness, disturbed sleep and liver affections; also as fomentation in painful menstruation.

―― 299 ――
MOUSE EAR. Gnaphalium Uliginosum.
Herb. . . . . . Sud. Sto. Muc.
Cud Weed. Dysentery Weed.
Used in coughs, diarrhœa and obstructions.

―― 300 ――
MUGWORT. Artemisia Vulgaris.
Herb. . . . . Dia. Emm. Ner.
Useful in epilepsy, hysteria, amenorrhea, promotes perspiration, increases the flow of urine and menses.

―― 301 ――
MULBERRY. Morus Rubra.
Bark. . . . . . Pur. Ant.
Fruit. . . . . . Ref. Lax.
Bark used to expel tape-worm; the berries are laxative and form a grateful drink after fevers, etc.

BOTANIC DRUGGISTS.

Per lb.

——— 302 ———
MULLEIN. Verbascum Thapsus.
    Herb. . . . . Dem. Diu. Ano. A-spa.
    Seed. . . . . Nar.
Bullock's Lungwort. Flannel Flower. Hares Beard. Hig Taper. Shepherd's Club. Woolen. Velvet Plant.
Used in cough, catarrh, diarrhœa, dysentery, piles, etc. also as a poultice in white-swellings, mumps, sore throat, etc.

——— 303 ———
MUSTARD, BLACK. Sinapis Nigra.
    Seed. . . . . Ves.

——— 304 ———
MUSTARD, WHITE. Sinapis Alba.
    Seed. . . . . . Sti. Rub. Ves.
The whole seed formerly used as a tonic in dyspepsia; ground is used as a condiment; in large doses acts as an emetic. Externally as poultice to rouse the system to activity, relieve pain and mitigate inflammation.

——— 305 ———
MYRRH. Balsamodendron Myrrha.
    Gum. . . . . . Sti. A-sep. Ver.
Myrrh is a stimulant to the mucous tissues and exerts an antiseptic influence; promotes expectoration and menstruation. Used in gleet, catarrh, bronchitis and asthma, also as poultice in sores, ulcers, sore throat, spongy gums, etc.

——— 306 ———
NANNY BUSH. Viburnum Lentago.
    Bark. . . . . A-per.
Black Thorn. Nanny Berry. Sheep Berry. Sweet Viburnum.

——— 307 ———
NEPHRITIC PLANT. Parthenium Integrifolium.
    Root. . . . . Diu.
Cutting Almond.
Highly extolled as a remedy in strangury, inflammation of the urinary passages and kidneys; also in amenorrhœa

——— 308 ———
NETTLE. Urtica Dioica.
    Herb. . . . . . Ast. Ton. Diu.
    Root. . . . . . " " "
Canada Nettle. Stinging Nettle.
Valuable in diarrhœa, dysentery, hemorrhoids, hemorrhages, gravel and scorbutic affections. The seeds reduce corpulence.

		Per lb.

——— 309 ———

NUTGALLS. Quercus Infectoria.
    Galls. . . . . Ast.
Dyers' Oak.
  Useful in dysentery, diarrhœa, passive hemorrhages, and as injection in gleet, leucorrhœa, prolapsus-ani, and as gargle in sore throat, canker, etc.

——— 310 ———

NUTMEGS. Myristica Fragrans.
    Fruit. . . . . . . Aro. Sti. Car.
Mace.
  Used for its fine flavor to correct the action of other medicines, to allay vomiting and nausea; charred with alum in intermittent fever.

——— 311 ———

NUX VOMICA. Strychnos Nux Vomica.
    Seeds. . . . . Nar. Poi.
Bachelor's Buttons. Columbrina. Dog Button. Ratsbane. False Angostura. Nux Metella. Poison Nut. Quaker Button.
  In medicinal doses, tonic, diaphoretic, laxative and diuretic. Should be used cautiously.

——— 312 ———

OAK BARK, BLACK. Quercus Nigra.   Ast.
"   "   **RED.**   "   Rubra.   "
"   "   **WHITE.**   "   Alba.   "
  Used in sore throat, offensive ulcers, obstinate chronic diarrhœa, hemorrhage, in gargles and injections, in leucorrhœa, prolapsus-ani and piles.

——— 313 ———

OAK OF JERUSALEM. Chenopodium Botrys.
    Herb. . . - . . . . Ant. A-spa.
    Seed. . . . .   "   "
American Wormseed. Goosefoot. Jerusalem Tea. Stinking Weed. Wormseed.
  Used to expel worms in children; also reputed beneficial in amenorrhœa.

——— 314 ———

ORANGE. Citrus Aurantium.
    Flowers. . . . . . . Aro. A-spa.
    Peel. . . . . Aro. Ton.
  Used to cover the taste of disagreeable medicines and lessen their tendency to nausea. The fruit after fevers where acids are craved, in scurvy, etc.

Per lb.

—— 315 ——
ORRIS, FLORENTINE. Iris Florentina.
  Root. . . . . . . Eme. Cat.
Used in the composition of tooth powders and to sweeten an offensive breath.

—— 316 ——
OSIER, GREEN. Cornus Circinata.
  Bark. . . . . Ast. Ton.
Alder-leaved Dogwood. Broad-leaved Dogwood, Green Ozier Dogachamus. Round,leaved Cornel. Kinnikinnick.
Useful in diarrhœa, dysentery, as a gargle in sore throat, also in typhoid fever and fever and ague.

—— 317 ——
OSIER, RED. Cornus Sericea.
  Bark. . . . . . . Ton. Ast. Sti.
Blueberry Cornel. Red Ozier. Rose Willow. Red Rod. Red Willow. Silky Cornel. Swamp Dogwood.
Valuable in dyspepsia, diarrhœa. and to check vomiting common to pregnancy, and disease of the uterus.

—— 318 ——
PALMA CHRISTI. Ricinus Communis.
  Seeds yield oil. . . . . . Cat.
  Leaves. . . . . Gal. Emm. F-com.
Castor Oil Plant.

—— 319 ——
PAREIRA BRAVA. Cissampelos Pareira.
  Root. . . . . . Ton. Diu. Alt.
Ice Vine. Velvet Leaf.
Used in chronic inflammation of the bladder, disorders of the urinary organs, leuccorrhœa, dropsy, jaundice, etc.

—— 320 ——
PARILLA YELLOW. Menispermum Canadense.
  Root. . . . . . . Ton. Lax. Alt.
Moonseed. Texas Sarsaparilla. Yellow Sarsaparilla. Vine Maple.
A superior laxative bitter, used in scrofula, syphilis, rheumatism, gout, and cutaneous diseases.

Per lb.

—— 321 ——
PARSLEY. Petroselinum Sativum.
    Leaves. . . . . . . Dem. Diu.
    Root. . . . . . Diu.
    Seed. . . . . . Car.
Root useful in dropsy, retention of urine, strangury and gonorrhœa. Leaves bruised, as fomentation, cures bites and stings of insects. Seed to destroy vermin in the hair.

—— 322 ——
PASSION FLOWER. Passiflora Incarnata.
    Herb. . . . . . . Sed. Ner.
Used for insomnia, neuralgia, epilepsy.

—— 323 ——
PEACH. Amygdalus Persica.
    Bark. . . . . . . Ton. Sto.
    Leaves. . . . . . "   "
    Pits, (Meats) . . . . "   "
Bark and meats (kernels) recommended in intermittent fever, leucorrhœa, dyspepsia jaundice, etc. The leaves in irritability of the bladder and urethra, inflammation of the stomach and abdomen.

—— 324 ——
PELLITORY. Anacyclus Pyrethrum.
    Root. . , ... Rub.
Pellitory of Spain. Spanish Chamomile.
Used for toothache, rheumatic and neuralgic affections of the head, palsy, etc.

—— 325 ——
PENNYROYAL. Hedeoma Pulegioides.
    Herb. . . . Abo. Sti. Dia. Emm. Car.
Squaw Mint. Stinking Balm. Thick Weed. Tick. Weed.
Promotes perspiration, restores suppressed lochia, excites the menstrual discharge, and is reported abortive.

—— 326 ——
PEONY. Pæonia Officinalis.
    Flowers. . . . . . A-spa. Ton. Ner.
    Root. . . . . . . "   "   "
Valuable in St. Vitus, epilepsy, spasms nervous diseases and whooping cough. Seeds reputed effective in preventing nightmare of dropsical persons.

BOTANIC DRUGGISTS. 63

Per lb.

—— 327 ——

PEPPER, BIRD. Capsicum Annuum Baccatum.
    Fruit. . . . . . . Sti. Cat. Rub.
Cayenne Pepper. Chillies. Chilly Pepper. Red Pepper. Spanish Pepper.
  A powerful stimulant used in colds, rheumatism, spasmodic affections and cholera.

—— 328 ——

PEPPER, BLACK. Piper Nigrum.
    Berry. . . . . . . Aro. Sti.
  A favorite condiment. Used in languid state of the stomach and bowels, dyspepsia, colic, and intermittents. The tincture to destroy lice, flies, etc.

—— 329 ——

PEPPER, WATER. Polygonum Hydropiper.
    Leaves. . . Acr. Pun. A-sep. Ape. Diu.
Arsmart. Biting. Knot Weed. Door Weed. Lake Weed. Smart Weed. Sickle Weed.
  Used in amenorrhœa gravel, colds, coughs, milk sickness, bowel complaints and erysipelas.

—— 330 ——

PEPPERMINT. Mentha Piperita.
    Herb. . . . . Sti. A-spa. Car. Sto.
  Used in flatulent colic, hysterics, spasm cramps in the stomach, allay nausea and vomiting; also to flavor other medicines.

—— 331 ——

PERUVIAN BARK. Cinchona Calisaya.
    Bark. . . . . Ton. Feb. A-per.
Jesuits' Bark.
  Valuable in all febrile, eruptive and inflammatory diseases of a periodic nature, and in general debility.

—— 332 ——

PICHI. Fabiana Imbricata.
    Herb. . . . . . . Diu. Ton.
Used in liver troubles, dyspepsia, etc.

Per lb.

—— 333 ——

PILEWORT. Amarantus Hypochondriacus.
      Herb. . . . . Ast.
Amaranth. Love Lies Bleeding. Princes' Feather. Red Cockscomb. Spleen Amaranth.
Recommended in severe menorrhagia, diarrhœa, dysentery, hemorrhage of the bowels, leucorrhæa, ulcers, etc.

—— 334 ——

PIMENTO. Eugenia Pimenta.
      Berries. . . . . Aro. Sti. Car.
Allspice. Clove Pepper. Jamaica Pepper.
Used to flavor other medicines. The tincture as a remedy for chilblains.

—— 335 ——

PINE, WHITE. Pinus Strobus.
      Bark. . . . . . Sti. Diu. Pec.
      Pitch. . . . . . Sti. Diu.
Used in cough, rheumatism, scurvy, kidney complaints. The pitch in gonorrhœa, gleet, fluor-albus, kidney and bladder complaints.

—— 336 ——

PINK. Spigelia Marilandica.
      Root. . . . . . . Sud. Ant.
American Worm Root. Carolina Pink. Indian Pink. Star Bloom. Worm Grass.
An active and certain vermifuge combined with Senna and Manna.

—— 337 ——

PIPSISSEWA. Chimaphila Umbellata.
      Herb. . . . . Diu. Ton. Alt. Ast.
Bitter Wintergreen. Ground Holly. King's Cure. Noble Pine. Princes' Pine. Pyrola. Pine Tulip. Wintergreen.
Useful in scrofula, chronic rheumatism, kidney diseases, strangury, gonorrhœa, catarrh of the bladder and cutaneous diseases.

BOTANIC DRUGGISTS. 65

| | Per lb. |

—— 338 ——

PLANTAIN. Plantago Major.
  Leaves. . . . . . Alt. Diu. A-sep
  Root. . . . . . " " "
Englishman's Foot. Round-leaved Plantain.
 Beneficial in syphilitic, mercurial and scrofulous diseases, leucorrhœa, diarrhœa, etc. The leaves in ointments.

—— 339 ——

PLEURISY ROOT. Asclepias Tuberosa.
  Root. . . . . . Diu. Car. Ton.
Butterfly Weed. Canada Root. Flux Root. Orange Swallow Wort. Tuber Root. Wind Root. White Root.
 In pleurisy, febrile diseases, flatulency, indigestion, acute rheumatism, dysentery, coughs, inflammation of the lungs, etc.

—— 340 ——

POISON OAK. Rhus Toxicodendron.
  Leaves. . . . . . Irritant Poison.
  Plant. . . . . Poi. Rub. Ves.
Climbing Sumach. Poison Vine. Poison Ivy. Trailing Sumach.
 Has been used in chronic paralysis, chronic rheumatism, cutaneous diseases, paraylsis of the bladder.

—— 341 ——

POLYPODY. Polypodium Vulgare.
  Root and Top. . . Pec. Dem. Pur. Ant.
Brake Root. Fern Root. Female Fern. Fern Brake. Rock Polypod. Rock Brake. Stone Brake.
 Used in pulmonary and hepatic complaints; also to expel worms.

—— 342 ——

POMEGRANATE. Punica Granatum.
  Rind of Fruit. . . . . Ast. Ton.
  Bark of Root. . . . Ast. Ant. F-com.
  Flowers. . . . " " "
Pomegranate Fruit. Punic Apple.
 Reputed valuable in removing tape worm, and in intermittent fever, night sweats, passive hemorrhages, diarrhœa, canker in the mouth, etc.

| | | Per lb. |

――― 343 ―――
POPLAR. Populus Tremuloides.
    Bark. . . . . Ton. Feb.
Aspen. Abele Tree. American Poplar. Quiver Leaf. Trembling Poplar. Trembling Tree. White Poplar.
Used in intermittent fever, emaciation and debility, impaired digestion, chronic diarrhœa, worms, gleet, etc.

――― 344 ―――
POPPY. Papaver Somniferum.
    Capsules. . . . . . Emo. Ano.
    Flowers. . . . . . Nar. Ano.
    Leaves. . . . . . " "
Valuable to promote rest, and as a poultice for painful swellings; the syrup given to restless children to procure sleep.

――― 345 ―――
PRAIRIE WEED. Silphium Gummiferum.
    Root. . . . . . . Eme. Feb.
    Gum. . . . . Diu.
Prairie Dock. Turpentine Sunflower.
Used in asthma.

――― 346 ―――
PRIVET. Ligustrum Vulgare.
    Flowers. . . . . Fra.
    Fruit. . . . . Cat.
    Leaves. . . . . . . Ast. Bit.
Primwort. Privy. Prim.

――― 347 ―――
PTELEA. Ptelea Trifoliata.
    Bark. . . . . . . Ton. Ast.
Ague Bark. Hop Tree. Prairie Grub. Pickaway Anise. Shrubby Trefoil. Stinking Ash. Stinking Prairie Bush. Wing Seed. Wafer Ash.
Recommended in intermittent and remittent fevers, asthma, pulmonary affections, indigestion and dyspepsia.

――― 348 ―――
PURPLE CONE FLOWER.
    Root. . . . . Alt.
Echinacea Angustifolia.
In syphilitic disorders.

――― 349 ―――
PULSATILLA. Anemone Pulsatilla.
    Herb. . . . Acr. Corrosive, Poi. Rub.
Meadow Anemone. Pasque Flower.

BOTANIC DRUGGISTS.

——— 350 ———
Per lb.

PUMPKIN. Cucurbita Pepo.
Seed, ... Muc. Diu.
Cold Seeds. Pompion.
Used in scalding of urine, affections of the urinary passages and said to remove tape-worm effectually.

——— 351 ———

QUASSIA. Simaruba Excelsa.
Wood. . . . . . . Ton. Feb. Ant.
Bitter Wood. Lofty Quassia. Mountain Damson. Bitter Ash. Stave Wood.
Used in remittent and intermittent fever, dyspepsia, general debility, worms, and to destroy the appetite for alcoholic drinks.

——— 352 ———

QUEEN OF THE MEADOW. Eupatorium Purpureum
. Herb. . . . . . . Diu. Sti. Ton.
Root. . . . . . . " " "
Gravel Root. Joepye. Kidney Root. Purple Boneset. Trumpet Weed,
A valuable remedy in dropsy, strangury, gravel and all urinary disorders.

——— 353 ———

QUEEN'S ROOT. Stillingia Sylvatica.
Root. . . . . . . Alt. Eme. Cat.
Cock-up-hat. Marcory. Queen's Delight. Stillingia. Silver Leaf. Yaw Root.
Invaluable in scrofula, syphilis, liver and cutaneous diseases, bronchitis, laryngitis and lung complaints.

——— 354 ———

QUERBRACO. Aspidosperma Quebracho.
Bark . . . . Ton.
Used for dyspepsia, asthma, bronchitis.

——— 355 ———

QUINCE. Cydonia Vulgaris.
Seed. . . . . . . Dem. Muc.
Very useful in gonorrhœa, dysentery, diarrhœa, aphthous affections, sore mouth and in ophthalmia as a collyrium.

——— 356 ———

RASPBERRY. Rubus Strigosus.
Leaves. . . . . Ast.
Red Raspberry.
An excellent remedy in diarrhœa, dysentery, cholera infantum, hemorrhage from the stomach, bowels or uterus, and as injection in gleet, leucorrhœa, canker, etc.

	Per lb.

––––– 357 –––––
RED GUM. Encalyptus Rostrata.
Bark. . . . . Ast.
An exudation from this and other species quite soluble in water, used to check purging, and in seasickness.

––––– 358 –––––
RED ROOT. Ceanothus Americana.
Bark. . . Ast. Exp. Sed. A-spa. A-syp.
New Jersey Tea. Mountain Sweet. Wild Snowball.
Used in gonorrhœa, dysentery, asthma, chronic bronchitis, whooping cough, and as gargle in canker, sore mouth, etc.

––––– 359 –––––
RHATANY. Krameria Triandria.
Root. . . . . Ast.
Employed in chronic diarrhœa, incontinence of urine hemorrhages, leucorrhœa, profuse menstruation, vomiting-blood, and in spongy gums to consolidate them and preserve the teeth.

––––– 360 –––––
RHUS AROMATICA.
Herb. . . . . Ast.
Useful in urinary troubles, diabetis, etc.

––––– 361 –––––
RHUBARB, AMERICAN. Rheum Rhaponticum.
Root. . . . . . Cat. Ton. Ast.
Said to possess the properties of foreign Rheum in a minor degree. Used for costiveness, debility, and summer complaint.

––––– 362 –––––
RHUBARB, INDIA. Rheum Palmatum.
Root. . . . . . . Cat. Ast. Ton.
Extensively used as a purgative, and in chronic diarrhœa, dysentery, convalescence from exhausting diseases when a mild cathartic is required, infantile complaints, dyspepsia, headache, etc.

––––– 363 –––––
ROCK BRAKE. Pteris Atropurpurea.
Herb. . . . . Ast. Ant.
Root. . . . . " "
Indian Dream. Winter Fern.
Efficacious in diarrhœa, dysentery, night sweats, to remove worms, and as vaginal injection in leucorrhœa, suppression of the lochia, etc.

BOTANIC DRUGGISTS.

Per lb.

—— 364 ——

ROSE FLOWERS, RED. Rosa Gallica.
" " **PALE.** Rosa Centifolia.

Rose flowers are tonic and mildly astringent. Used in hemorrhages, excessive mucous discharges and bowel complaints; the infusion with pith of Sassafras for inflammation of the eyes, etc.

—— 365 ——

ROSEMARY. Rosmarinus Officinalis.
    Leaves. . . . . . Sti. A-spa. Emm.

The warm infusion for colds, colic and nervous conditions. The oil in liniments and plasters an external stimulant.

—— 366 ——

ROSIN WEED. Silphium Laciniatum.
    Plant . . . . Eme. Feb.

Compass Plant Weed. Polar Plant. Pilot Weed.
Heaves in horses.

—— 367 ——

RUE. Ruta Graveolens.
    Herb. . . . Ant. Sti. Emm. A-spa.

Countryman's Treacle.

A narcotic-acrid poison, causing abortion and miscarriage in females. Medicinally, has been used in flatulent colic, hysterics, epilepsy, and as a vermifuge.

—— 368 ——

RUSH, SCOURING. Equisetum Hyemale.
    Stalks. . . . . Diu. Ast.

Dutch Rush. Gunbright. Horse-tail Rush. Horse Pipe. Pewterwort. Polishing Rush.

The infusion used for voiding bloody urine, suppression of urine, dropsy, gonorrhœa, gleet, etc.

—— 369 ——

RYE, SPURRED. Sclerotium Clavus.
    Fungus. . . Poi. Emm. Par. Abo. F-com.

Ergot.

—— 370 ——

SABADILLA. Veratum Officinale.
    Seed. . . . . . . Poi. Ant. Ins.

Cevadella.

Used for rheumatism.

|Per lb.

―― 371 ――

SAFFRON. Carthamus Tinctorius.
      Flowers. . . . . . Emm. Dia.
American Saffron. Bastard Saffron. Dyers' Saffron. False Saffron.
  Has been used beneficially in amenorrhœa, dysmenorrhœa, chlorosis hysteria, suppression of the lochial discharges, febrile diseases, scarlet fever, measles, etc.

―― 372 ――

SAGE. Salvia Officinalis.
      Herb. . . . . . Ton. Ast. Exp. Dia.
  Valuable in cough, colds, night sweats, worms, spermatorrhœa, and as gargle for ulcerated sore throat; also to produce perspiration.

―― 373 ――

SAGE, WOOD. Teucrium Canadensis.
      Leaves. . . . . Sti. Aro. Ton.
Germander.
  Used in infusion for fevers, rheumatism, gout, chlorosis, etc.

―― 374 ――

SANICLE, AMERICAN. Heuchera Americana.
      Root. . . . . . Powerful Ast.
Alum Root. Ground Maple.

―― 375 ――

SANICLE, BLACK. Sanicula Marilandica.
      Root. . . . . . Ner. Ano. Ast.
Black Snakeroot.
  Resembles Valerian. Used in chorea, erysipelas, dysentery, fluor-albus, etc.

―― 376 ――

SANICLE, WHITE. Eupatorium Aromaticum.
      Root. . . . . Dia. A-spa. Exp. Aro.
Pool Root. Poolwort. White Snakeroot.
  Used in ague, stomach complaints, nervous diseases and pulmonary affections.

Per lb.

—— 377 ——
SARSAPARILLA, AMERICAN. Aralia Nudicaulis.
" **SPANISH.** Smilax Officinalis.
   Root. . . . . . . Alt. Diu.
False Sarsaparilla.   Rabbits' Root.   Small Spikenard.
 Wild Licorice.   Wild Sarsaparilla.
 Used in chronic diseases of the skin, rheumatic affections, dropsy, veneral complaints, and in all cases where alteratives are required.

—— 378 ——
SASSAFRAS. Sassafras Variifolium.
   Bark. . . . . Diu. Aro. Sti. Alt. Diu.
   Pith. . . . . . . Dem. Muc.
Ague Tree.   Cinnamon Wood.   Saloop Saxifrax.
 Valuable in scrofula and eruptive diseases, and as a flavor. The pith used as an eye wash in ophthalmia and as a drink in disorders of the chest, bowels, kidneys and bladder.

—— 379 ——
SAUNDERS, RED. Pterocarpus Santalinus.
   Wood. . . . . . . Ton. Ast.
Red Wood.
 Used only in coloring tinctures, etc.

—— 380 ——
SAVIN. Juniperus Sabina.
   Leaves. . . . . Emm. Diu. Dia. Ant.
 Used in kidney complaints, suppression of urine and obstructed menstruation.

—— 381 ——
SAXIFRAGE. Pimpinella Saxifraga.
   Root. . . . Aro. Nau. Pun. Sti. Sto.
Small Burnet Saxifrage. Small Saxifrage. Small Pimpernel.

—— 382 ——
SCABIOUS, SWEET. Erigeron Philadelphicum.
   Flowers. . . . Diu. Ast. Ton. Dia. Emm.
Mourning Bride.   Mourning Widow.   Philadelphia Fleabane.   Skevish.

	Per lb.

—— 383 ——

SCABISH. Œnothera Biennis.
      Herb. . . . . . . Vul. Muc.
Evening Primrose. Tree Primrose.
  Valuable in cough, tetter and eruptive diseases.

SCABISH. Œnothera Glauca.
      Plant. . . . . . . Exa. Emo. Det.
Sundrops.

—— 384 ——

SCROFULA PLANT. Scrophularia Marilandica.
      Herb. . . . . Deo. Alt. Diu. Ano.
Carpenter's Square. Figwort. Figwort Herb. Healall. Holmes' Weed. Square Stalk.
  Valuable in scrofula, cutaneous diseases, dropsy, ulcers, etc.

—— 385 ——

SCULLCAP. Scutellaria Lateriflora.
      Herb. . . . . . Ton. Ner. A-spa.
Blue Scullcap. Hoodwort. Helmet Flower. Mad-dog-weed. Blue Pimpernel. Side-flowering Scullcap. Madweed. Hooded Willow Herb.
  Valuable in all nervous complaints, chorea, wakefulness, delirium tremens, convulsions, excitability etc.

—— 386 ——

SCURVY GRASS. Cochlearia Officinalis.
      Herb. . . . . A-sco. Sti. Dia. Diu.
Scrubby Grass. Spoonwort.
  Valuable in scurvy and obstructions, dropsy, paralysis and rheumatism.

—— 387 ——

SEA WRACK. Fucus Versiculosus.
      Yields kelp.
Fucus. Bladder Wrack.
  Used in obesity.

—— 388 ——

SENNA, AMERICAN. Cassia Marilandica.
      Leaves. . . . . . . Cat. Deo.
Locust Plant. Wild Senna.
  A valuable cathartic, mild and effectual.

Per lb.

—— 389 ——

SENNA, ALEXANDRIAN. Cassia Acutifolia.
    " **INDIA.**   " Elongata.
      Leaves. . . . . Cat.
A certain and covenient cathartic, and may be used in all cases where a physic is required. The griping may be modified by ginger or cloves added.

—— 390 ——

SHAG-BARK TREE. Carya Alba.
      Bark. . . . . Cat.
      Fruit. . . . . Esc.
      Leaves. . . . . . . Mild Ast.
Ackroot. Hickory Tree. Shag-bark Walnut. Walnut.
  Used in scrofula, debility, diarrhœa, and as a gentle cathartic; as a wash for ulcers and sore eyes.

—— 391 ——

SHAMROCK. Oxalis Acetosella.
      Plant. . . . . . Aci. Ref. Diu. A-sco.
Cuckoo Bread. Sour Trefoil. Wood Sorrel.

—— 392 ——

SHEPHERDS' PURSE. Capsella Bursa-pastoris.
      Herb. . . . . . . Acr. Det. Ast.
Cocowort. Pickpocket. Pickpurse. Poor Man's Pharmacetty. Toywort.
  Used with Yarrow to check profuse menstruation and hemorrhage.

—— 393 ——

SHEPHERDS' WEATHERGLASS. Anagallis Arvensis.
      Plant. . . . A-ven. Poi. Ner. Exp. Sti.
Red Chickweed. Scarlet Pimpernel.

—— 394 ——

SHOVEL WEED. Unisema Deltifolia.
      Root. . . . . . Emo. Ast. Det.
      Seed. . . . . Far.
Pickerel Weed.

—— 395 ——

SMILAX, BOSTON. Myrsiphyllum Asparagoides.
      Plant. . . . . Orn. Decorative.
Cape Smilax.

—— 396 ——
SNAKEROOT, BUTTON. Liatris Spicata.
Root. . . . . . Diu. Ton. Emm.
Backache Root. Devil's Bit. Gayfeather. Prairie Pine. Rough Root. Sawwort. Throatwort.

Valuable in scrofula, dysmenorrhœa, amenorrhœa, gleet, etc.; also in Bright's disease, combined with Bugle and Unicorn.

Per lb

—— 397 ——
SNAKEROOT, CANADA. Asarum Canadense.
Root. . . . . . Sti. Aro. Dia.
Broad-leaved Asarabacca. Coltsfoot Snakeroot. Catfoot. Heart Snakeroot. Indian Ginger. Southern Snakeroot. Vermont Snakeroot. Wild Ginger. False Coltsfoot.

Valuable in causing perspiration, promotes expectoration, and possesses carminative properties. Used in colic, etc.

—— 398 ——
SNAKEROOT, RATTLE. Goodyera Pubescens.
Herb. . . . . . . A-sco.
Adder's Violet. Networt. Net-leaf Plantain. Spotted Plantain. Rattlesnake Leaf.

Reputed to have cured scrofula; also used in leucorrhœa, proplapsus-uteri, and as a wash in scrofulous ophthalmia.

—— 399 ——
SNAKEROOT, SAMPSON. Gentiana Ochroleuca.
Root. . . . Bit. Ton. Ant. Ast. A-bil. Feb.
Employed to invigorate the stomach and digestive organs, hectic and nervous fevers, gout and rheumatism.

—— 400 ——
SNAKEROOT, SENEGA. Polygala Senega.
Root. . . Sia. Exp. Diu. Eme. Cat. Emm.
Mountain Flax. Seneca Root. Seneka Snakeroot. Senega Root.

In chronic catarrh, croup, asthma and lung diseases.

—— 401 ——
SNAKEROOT, VIRGINIA. Aristolochia Serpentaria.
Root. . . . . . Sti. Ton. Dia.
Birthwort. Pelican Flower. Sangrel. Snakeweed. Sangree Root. Thick Birthwort.

To produce perspiration, strengthen the stomach, appetite, etc.

BOTANIC DRUGGISTS.

Per lb.

——— 402 ———
SNEEZEWORT. Achillea Ptarmica.
Root. . . . . Acr.
Leaves. . . . . . Ste. Pun.
German Pellitory. Bastard Pellitory.

——— 403 ———
SOAP TREE. Quillaya Saponaria.
Bark. . . . . Sap. Feb.
Quillai Bark. Quillaya.
Used in preparations for cleansing the hair, and as a snuff for cold in the head; also as febrifuge.

——— 404 ———
SOAPWORT. Saponaria Officinalis.
Herb. . . . . . . Ton. Dia. Alt.
Bruisewort. Bouncing Bet. Fullers' Herb. Old Maid's Pink. Sheep Weed.
Valuable in syphilis, scrofula, cutaneous diseases, jaundice, liver complaints, etc.

——— 405 ———
SOLOMON, SEAL. Convallaria Multiflora.
Root. . . . . . Ton. Muc. Ast.
Dropberry. Giant Solomon Seal. Sealwort. Seal Root.
Much used in female debility, leucorrhœa, piles, and pectoral affections, erysipelas, and as a wash in poison from ivy, etc.

——— 406 ———
SOURWOOD. Oxydendrum Arboreum.
Bark. . . . . Ton. Diu.
Used in dropsy.

——— 407 ———
SOLOMON SEAL, SMALL. Convallaria Racemosa.
Root. . . . Ast. Ton. Muc. Exp. F-com.

——— 408 ———
SORREL, MOUNTAIN. Oxyria Reniformis.
Leaves. . . . . Diu. Ref.

——— 409 ———
SORREL, SHEEP. Rumex Acetosella.
Leaves. . . . . Diu. Ref.
Cuckoo Bread. Wood Sorrel.
Used in scurvy, scrofula and skin diseases. As poultice to tumors, wens, boils, etc., and an extract said to cure cancers and tumors.

Per lb.

—— 410 ——

SOUTHERNWOOD. Artemisia Abrotanum.
   Herb. . . . . Sti. Ner. Ton. Ant.
Boy's Love. Lad's Love. Old Man. Sloven wood.
 Valuable in obstructions, and to remove worms.

—— 411 ——

SPEARMINT. Mentha Viridis.
   Herb. . . . . A.-spa. Car. Sti. Diu.
 Valuable in colic, spasms, dropsy, and to prevent vomiting, gravel, suppression of urine, scalding of urine, and as local application to piles.

—— 412 ——

SPEEDWELL. Veronica Officinalis.
   Herb. . . . . Exp. Alt. Ton. Diu.
Virginia Speedwell.
 Recommended in croup, catarrh, renal and skin diseases, jaundice, scrofula, etc.

—— 413 ——

SPIKENARD. Aralia Racemosa.
   Root. . . . . Pec. Sto.
American Spikenard. Indian Root. Life-of-man. Spignet. Petty Morrel.
 Used in coughs, colds, pulmonary affections, gout, skin diseases, and to purify the blood.

—— 414 ——

SPLEENWORT. Asplenium Adiantum.
   Herb. . . . . . . Dem. Pec.
Used in pectoral and lung diseases.

—— 415 ——

SPUNK. (Species of Agaric.) Boletus Fomentarius.
   Plant. . . . . . Sty. Ast. Bit.
Oak Agaric.

—— 416 ——

SPURGE, BLACK. Euphorbia Maculata.
   Leaves. . . . . . Ast. Ton. Nar.
Spotted Spurge.

—— 417 ——

SPURGE, BLOOMING. Euphorbia Corollata.
      Root. . . . . . . Eme. Dia. Exp.
Emetic Root. Large Flowering Spurge. Milk Pursley. Milkweed. Milk Ipecac. Milk Purslain. Picac. Hippo. Purging Root. Snake Milk. White Pursley. White Purslain.
Valuable in dropsy.

—— 418 ——

SPURGE, LARGE SPOTTED. Euphorbia Hypericifolia.
      Leaves. . . . . . . Ast. Ton. Nar.

—— 419 ——

SQUAW VINE. Mitchella Repens.
      Herb. . . . . . Par. Diu. Ast.
Deer Berry. Hive Vine. One Berry. Partridge Berry. Winter Clover.
Highly beneficial in diseases of the uterus, parturition, dropsy, suppression of urine; a powerful uterine tonic.

—— 420 ——

SQUILL. Scilla Maritima.
      Root. (bulb) . . . Exp. Diu. Cat. Eme.
Sea Onion.
Sometimes used in dropsy, and as an expectorant in chronic catarrh, pneumonia, asthma, phthisic and other bronchial affections.

—— 421 ——

STAPHISAGRIA. Delphinium Staphisagria.
(Stavesacre)
      Seed. . . . . . . Poi. Emm. Nar.
Used to kill vermin.

—— 422 ——

STONE ROOT. Collinsonia Canadensis.
      Root. and Plant. . . . . . . Sti.
Horse Balm. Horse Weed. Hardhack. Healall. Knob Grass. Knob Root. Ox Balm. Richweed.
Used in chronic catarrh of the bladder, fluor-albus and debility of the stomach, lithic acid, calculous deposits, etc.

Per lb.

——— 423 ———

STORAX BARK. Liquidambar Orientale.
       Gum. . . . Aro. Fragrant, Bal. Sti. Exp.
Sweet Gum Bark.

——— 424 ———

STROPHANTHUS. Strophanthus Hispidus.
       Seeds. . . . . Poi.
Used in heart troubles.

——— 425 ———

STRAWBERRY. Fragaria Vesca (Virginiana.)
       Leaves. . . . . . Ast. Feb. Ref.
Useful in diarrhœa, dysentery, intestinal debility and night sweats. The fruit in calculous disorders and gout.

——— 426 ———

SUMACH. Rhus Glabrum.
       Bark. . . . . . Ton. Ast. A-sep.
       Berries. . . . . Ref Diu.
       Leaves. . . . . Ton. Ast. A-sep.
Pennsylvania Sumach. Smooth Sumach. Upland Sumach. Valuable in gonorrhœa, leucorrhœa, diarrhœa, hectic fever and scrofula. The berries in diabetes, bowel complaint, febrile diseases, canker, sore mouth, etc.

——— 427 ———

SUMBUL. Euryangium Sumbul.
       Root. . . . . . Aro. Bal. Sti. Ton.
Musk Root.

——— 428 ———

SUMMER SAVORY. Satureja Hortensis.
       Herb. . . . . . Sti. Car. Emm
Beneficial in colds, menstrual suppression, flatulent colic, and as a gentle, stimulating tonic after fevers. The oil used to relieve toothache.

BOTANIC DRUGGISTS. 79

Per lb.

—— 429 ——

SUNDEW. Drosera Rotundifolia.
    Plant. . . . Acr. Det. Rub. Pec. Aph.
Round-leaved Sundew. Youthwort.

—— 430 ——

SUNFLOWER. Helianthus Annuus.
    Seed. . . . . . . Exp. Diu.
Comb Flower. Garden Sunflower.
    Used in cough and pulmonary affections, dysentery, inflammation of the bladder and kidneys. The leaves are astringent.

—— 431 ——

SUNFLOWER, SWAMP. Helenium Autumnale.
    Flowers. . . . . . . Err.
    Herb. . . . . Ton. Dia. Err. Feb.
Sneezwort. False Sunflower.

—— 432 ——

SWEET FLAG. Acorus Calamus.
    Root. . . . . . Car. Sto. Sti.
Calamus. Grass Myrtle. Myrtle Flag. Sweet Flagroot. Sweet Myrtle. Sweet Sedge. Sweet Root. Sweet Cane. Sweet Rush.
    Used in flatulent colic dyspepsia, feeble digestion, and to aid the action of Peruvian Bark in intermittents. Externally to excite the discharges from blistered surfaces, indolent ulcers and issues.

—— 433 ——

TAMARACK. Larix Americana.
    Bark. . . . . Lax. Ton. Diu. Alt.
    Gum-resin. . . . . . . C-irr.
American Larch. Black Larch. Hackmatac. Larch.
    Recommended in obstructions of the liver, rheumatism, jaundice and cutaneous diseases.

—— 434 ——

TANSY. Tanacetum Vulgare.
    Herb. . . . . . Ton. Emm. Dia.
Double Tansy. Double-flowered Tansy. Hindheel.
    In fevers, agues, hysterics, dropsy, worms, and as fomentation in swellings, tumors, inflammation, etc.

—— 435 ——
THIMBLEWEED. Rudbeckia Laciniata.
   Herb. . . . . . . Diu. Ton. Bal.
Cone Disk. Cone Flower.
 Valuable in Bright's disease, wasting of the kidneys, and urinary complaints generally.

—— 436 ——
THISTLE ROOT. Cirsium Arvensis.
   Root. . . . . Ton. Ast
Blessed Thistle. Canada Thistle. Cursed Thistle. Holy Thistle.
 Boiled with milk for dysentery and diarrhœa.

—— 437 ——
THORN-APPLE. Datura Stramonium.
   Leaves (poisonous) . . . A-spa. Nar. Sed.
   Seeds " . . A-spa. Nar. Anti-Abo.
Apple Peru. Jamestown Weed. Jimson Weed. Mad Apple. Stickwort.
 In epilepsy, tic-douloureux and nervous affections, ophthalmic operations, etc. The leaves smoked to relieve spasmodic asthma. The seeds to prevent abortion.

—— 438 ——
THYME. Thymus Vulgaris.
   Herb. . . . . Ton. Car. Emm. A-spa.
Used in dyspepsia, weak stomach, hysteria, dysmenorrhœa, flatulence, colic, headache and to produce perspiration.

——439——
TORMENTILLA. Potentilla Tormentilla.
   Root. . . . . Ast. Ton.
Septfoil. Shepherd's Knot.
 Used in chronic diarrhœa, dysentery, passive hemorrhages, as an astringent injection, and as a local application to flabby ulcers.

—— 440 ——
TOUCH WOOD. Polyporus Ignarius.
   Plant. . . . . . Sty. Ast. Bit.
Agaric. Punk.

—— 441 ——
TREE OF HEAVEN. Ailanthus Glandulosus.
   Bark. . . , . . Anth. Anti-neuro.
 Used in diarrhœa and dysentery, hiccough, &c.

Per lb.

BOTANIC DRUGGISTS.

Per lb.

—— 442 ——

TURKEY CORN. Corydalis Formosa.
    Root. . . . . Ton. Alt. Diu.
Dielytra. Stagger-weed. Turkey Pea.
  One of the best remedies in syphilitic diseases, also in scrofula and cutaneous affections.

—— 443 ——

TURMERIC ROOT. Curcuma Longa.
    Root. . . . . Aro. Sti.
Curcuma.
  Used to color tinctures and ointments; also as a test for alkalies which turn it red or brown.

—— 444 ——

TWIN-LEAF. Jeffersonia Diphylla.
    Root. . . . . Sti. Dia. Diu. Alt. A-spa.
Ground Squirrel Pea. Helmet Pod. Rheumatism Root.
  Successfully used in chronic rheumatism, secondary syphilis, mercurial syphilis, dropsy and nervous affections, spasms, cramps, etc.; as gargle in diseases of the throat, scarlatina and indolent ulcers.

—— 445 ——

UNICORN. Helonias Dioica.
    Root. . . Alt. Emm. F-com. Ton. Diu. Ver.
Drooping Starwort. False Unicorn. Reed Seed. Unicorns' Horn.
  Invaluable as a uterine tonic, imparting tone and vigor to the reproductive organs; used in leucorrhœa, amenorrhœa, dysmenorrhœa, and to remove the tendency to miscarriage.

—— 446 ——

UVA URSI. Arctostaphylos Uva Ursi.
    Leaves. . . . . . . Ton. Diu. Ast.
    Berries. . . . . Ton. Ast.
Bearberry. Bears' Grape. Kinnikinnick. Mountain Box. Mountain Cranberry. Meal Berry. Sagackhomi. Upland Cranberry. Universe Vine.
  Used in chronic affections of the kidneys and urinary passages, strangury, diabetes, fluor-albus, and excessive mucous discharges with the urine, lithic acid, etc.

—— 447 ——
VALERIAN, ENGLISH. Valeriana Officinalis.
    Root. . . . . . . Ton. Ner.   Per lb.
All Heal. American English Valerian. Officinal Valerian. Setwall. Vandal Root.
  Used in chorea, nervous debility, hysteria and low forms of fever where a nervous stimulant is required.

—— 448 ——
VERVAIN. Verbena Hastata.
    Herb. . . . . . Ton. Eme. Exp. Sud.
American Vervain. Blue Vervain. False Vervain. Purvain. Simpler's Joy. Traveller's Joy. Wild Hyssop.
  Used in intermittents, colds, obstructed menses, scrofula, gravel, worms, etc.

—— 449 ——
VIOLET, BLUE. Viola Pedata.
    Herb. . . . . Muc. Emo. Lax. A-syp.
Birdsfoot Violet.
  Used in colds, cough, sore throat, etc.

—— 450 ——
VIOLET, CANKER. Viola Rostrata.
    Herb. . . . . . . Muc. Emm. Lax.
    Plant. . . . . . . Pec. Eme.
Beaked Violet.
  Said to be useful in pectoral and cutaneous diseases, also in syphilis.

—— 451 ——
VIRGINIA STONE CROP. Penthorum Sedoides.
  . . . . Ast. Dem. Lax.
Dutch. Dutch Stone Crop.
  Used in nasal catarrh.

—— 452 ——
VIRGIN'S-BOWER. Clematis Virginica.
    Leaves. . . . . . . Sti. Ner.
  Used in severe headache, cancerous ulcers, and as ointment in itch.

—— 453 ——
WAHOO. Euonymus Atropurpureus.
    Bark. . . . . Ton. Lax. Alt. Diu. Exp.
    Seed. . . . . Cat.
Arrow Wood. Burning Bush. Bitter Ash.
  Useful in intermittents, dyspepsia, torpid liver, constipation, dropsy and pulmonary affections.

BOTANIC DRUGGISTS.

Per lb.

——— 454 ———

WATER CUP. Sarracenia Purpurea.
    Herb. . . . . Ton. Sti. Diu. Lax.
Eve's Cup. Flytrap. Forefathers' Cup. Huntsman's Cup. Pitcher Plant. Side-saddle Plant. Side-saddle Flower. Smallpox Plant.
  Used in chlorosis, all uterine derangements, dyspepsia and gastric difficulties; said to be useful in smallpox.

——— 455 ———

WATERMELON. Vulgaris Citrullus.
    Seed. . . . . . . Muc. Diu.
Cold Seeds.
  Valuable in strangury and other urinary affections, dropsy, etc.

——— 456 ———

WHITE WOOD. Liriodendron Tulipifera.
    Bark. . . . . . A-per. Ton. Sti.
Canoe Wood. Lyre Tree. Tulip Tree. Tulip Poplar. White Poplar. Wild Poplar. Yellow Poplar.
  Useful in intermittent fever, low condition of the system dyspepsia, diarrhœa, hysteria, etc.

——— 457 ———

WHORTLEBERRY. Vaccinium Corymbosum.
    Fruit. . . . . . . Diu. Ast.
Bilberry. Black Whortleberry. Huckleberry.
  A valuable diuretic. The bark for gargle in sore mouth.

——— 458 ———

WICKUP. Epilobium Angustifolium.
    Herb and Root. . . . . . Ast.
Indian Wicopy. Marestail. Willow Herb. Wicopy Herb.
  Used in dysentery, diarrhœa, and where an astringent is required.

——— 459 ———

WILLOW, PUSSY. Salix Nigra.
    Bark. . . . . . Ton. Ast. Ant.
    Catkins. . . . . . Ton. Aph.
  Used in indigestion, in weak and relaxed condition of the bowels, diarrhœa, worms, gangrene, indolent ulcers, etc. The catkins as an aphrodisiac.

—— 460 ——	Per lb.

WILLOW, SAGE. Lythrum Salicaria.
 Bark. . . . . Ast.
 Herb. . . . . Muc. Ast. Dem. A-syp.
Loose Strife. Purple Willow Herb. Rainbow Weed.
Used for canker in the mouth, stomach and bowels.

—— 461 ——

WILLOW, WHITE. Salix Alba.
 Bark. . . . . . ;Ton. A-per. Ast.
Used in intermittent fever, debility of the digestive organs, hemorrhages, chronic mucous discharges, diarrhœa and dysentery.

—— 462 ——

WINTERGREEN, SPOTTED. Chimaphila Maculata.
 Plant. . . Diu. Ton. Alt. Ast. Exa. A-syp.
Spotted Pipsissewa.

—— 463 ——

WINTER'S BARK. Drymis. Winteri.
 Bark. . . . . . Sti. Aro. Ton. A-sco.
Used in scurvy, weakened digestion, low fevers, fever and ague, etc.

—— 464 ——

WITCH HAZEL. Hamamelis Virginica.
 Bark. . . . . . Ton. Ast. Sed.
 Leaves. . . . . . " " "
Pistachio. Snapping Hazel. Spotted Alder. Striped Alder. Wood Tobacco. Winter Bloom.
Valuable in diarrhœa, dysentery, excessive mucous discharges, etc., as a wash in painful swellings, gargle for canker, injection for fluor-albus.

—— 465 ——

WORMWOOD. Artemisia Absinthium.
 Herb. . . . . . Ant. Ton. Nar.
Absinthium.
Used in intermittent fever, jaundice and worms; also to promote the appetite. Externally in bruises and inflammations.

—— 466 ——

WORMWOOD, ROMAN. Ambrosia Artemisiæfolia.
 Herb. . . . . . . Emo. A-sep.
Hogweed. Ragweed. Stammerwort.
Used in fomentation in wounds and bruises, and as ointment in piles, ulces, to reduce painful swellings, etc.

Per lb.

—— 467 ——

YAM, WILD. Dioscorea Villos
    Root. . . . . A-spa.
Colic Root. China Root. Devil's Bones.
  Successfully used in bilious colic, spasms, cramps, flatulence, after-pains, affections of the liver, etc.

—— 468 ——

YARROW. Achillea Millefolium.
    Herb. . . . . . Ast. Alt. Diu.
Milfoil. Nosebleed.
  Used in hemorrhages, incontinuence of urine, diabetes, piles, dysentery, flatulence, and as injection in leucorrhœa.

—— 469 ——

YELLOW ROOT. Xanthorhiza Apiifolia.
    Root. . . . . Ton.
Shrub Yellow Root.
  A pure bitter tonic, and may be used for all purposes where simple bitter tonics are applicable.

—— 470 ——

YERBA SANTA. Eriodyction Glutinosum & Californicum.
    Bear's Weed. . . . . Pec. Ton. Muc.
Consumptives' Weed. Holy Herb. Mountain Balm.
  Useful in chronic laryngitis and bronchitis, in nasal catarrh and rheumatism.

INDEX.

∗ The numbers refer to the paragraph not the page.

Aaron's Beard	1	Alder, Red	14
Abele Tree	343	" Smooth	14
Abscess Root	2	" Spotted	464
Absinthium	465	" Striped	13, 464
Ackroot	390	" Swamp	13
Aconite	3	" Tag	14, 15
Acrid Lettuce	264	" White	16
Adam and Eve	4	Ale Cost	146
Adam's Apple	5	" Hoof	247
Adder's Mouth	119	Alkanet	17
" Leaf	6	" Dyers'	17
" Tongue	6	All Heal	447
Adonis Vernalis	7	Allspice	334
Agaric	440	Almond, Cutting	307
" Larch	8	Aloe, American	9
" Oak	415	" False	10
" of the Oak	8	" Root	61
" Purging	8	Alum Root	150, 374
" White	8	Amaranth	333
Agave, American	9	Amazon Root	197
" Virginian	10	Ambrosia, Tall	230
Agrimony	11	Anemone, Meadow	349
" Hemp	12	Angelica	18
Ague Bark	347	" American	18
" Grass	61	" High	18
" Root	61	" Purple	18
" Tree	378	" Tree	169
" Weed	66	Angostura	19
Alder, American	15	" False	311
" Black	13	Angustura	19
" Brook	13	Anise, Common	20
" Common	15	" Root	123
" False	13	" Seed	20

BOTANIC DRUGGISTS.

Antimony, Vegetable	66
Apple, Hog.	283
" Indian	66
" May	283
" Peru	437
" Tree Bark	21
Arabian Balsam of Gilead	36
Arbor Vitæ	22
Arbutus, Trailing	208
Archangel	18
" Green	79
" Purple	80
Areca Nut	23
" Palm	23
Arnica	24
Arrow Wood	25
" " Indian	69
Arsmart	329
Asarabacca, Broad-leaved	397
Ash Berries, Prickly	28
" Bitter	356, 453
" Black	26
" Mountain	27
" Poison	194
" Prickly	28
" Southern Prickly	29, 169
" Sea	29
" Stinking	347
" Wafer	347
" White	30
Asparagus	31
Aspen	343
Aster	132
" Red-stalked	132
Asthma Weed	275
Astringent Root	32, 150
Avens Root	32
" Purple	32
" Water	32
" White	32
Bachelor's Buttons	84, 311
Backache Brake	33
" Root	396
Badgersbane	3
Balm, Bastard	34
" Bee	35, 37
" Blue	37
" Field	105
" Indian	51
" Lemon	37
" Mountain	35, 470
" of Gilead	36
" of Gilead Herb	39
" Red	35
" Stinking	325
" Sweet	39
Balmony	38
" East India	122
Balsam of Canada	186
" Fir	186
" of Fir	186
" Seaside	102
" Sweet	267
" Weed	108, 267
" White	267
Baneberry	136
" Red	135
" White	136
Barberry	40
Bardana	81
Bardane	81
Basil, Common	41
" Sweet	41
" Wild	162
Basswood	42, 272
Bastard Bear's Foot	218
Bast Tree	42
Bayberry	43
Bay Bush Buds	179
Bay, Sweet	44
Bead Tree	45
Bean Trefoil	75
Beaked Violet	450
Bearbane	3
Bearberry	446
Bear's Bed	212
" Foot	46, 218
" Grape	446
Bear's paw Root	178

Bear's Weed	470	Bitter Root	56
Beastsbane	3	" Stem	122
Beaumont Root	60	" Stick	122
Beaver Poison	124	Bittersweet, Climbing	57
" Root	271	" False	57
" Tree	279	" Twigs	58
Beccabunga	70	Bitter Trefoil	75
Bedeguar	165	" Wintergreen	337
Bedstraw	126	" Wood	351
Beech Drops	89	Bitterworm	75
" Tree	47	Bitterwort	200
Bee's nest Plant	99	Blackberry	59
Beggars' Tick	153	Black Root	60
Beggars' Tick, Swamp	48	" Thorn	306
Belladonna	49	Bladder Podded Lobelia	275
Bellwort	50		
" Large-flowered	50	Bladder Wrack	387
Bellyache Root	18	Blazing Star	61
Benjamin Bush	181	Bleeding Heart	297
Bennet	32	Blessed Thistle	98, 436
Betel-nut Tree	23	Blister Weed	84
Beth Root	51	Blood Root	62
Betony	52	" Staunch	191
" Water	54	Bloodwort	63
" Wood	52	" Striped	63
Bilberry	457	Blue Bells	2, 201
Bindweed	284	" Berry	134
Birch, Black	53	Blueberry Cornel	317
" Cherry	53	Blue Flag	64
" Mahogany	53	Blue Gum Tree	184
" Sweet	53	" Mallows	281
Bird's Nest Root	99, 188	Bog Bean	75
Bird Weed	255	Boldo	65
Birth Root	51	Boneset	66
Birthwort	401	" Purple	352
" Thick	401	Bookoo	74
Bistort	55	Borage	67
Bishop's Leaves	54	Bouncing Bet	404
Biting Knot Weed	329	Bowman's Root	60
Biting Stone Crop	233	Box	68
Bitter Apple	138	" Berry	115
" Bark	192	" False	69
" Bloom	110	" Garden Edging	68
" Clover	110	Boxwood	69
" Gourd	138	Boy's Love	410
" Herb	38	Brake, Buckhorn	76

Brake, Fern	76, 341	Burr Seed	81
" Flowering	76	" Thistle	127
" Rock	363, 341	" Weed	127
" Root	341	Burrwort	84
" Sweet	178	Butter Bur	141
Brandybottles	271	Buttercup	84
Brinton Root	60	Butterfly Weed	339
British Tobacco	141	Butternut	85
Broad-Leaved Kalmia	260	Butter Weed	191
Brook Bean	75		
Brooklime	70	Cabbage, Skunk	86
Broom	71	Cactus	87
" Flowers	71	" Night-blooming	87
" Indigo	243	Calamba Root	140
" Irish	71	Calamint	88
Broomrape	81	Calamus	432
Broom, Yellow	243	Calico Bush	260
Bruisewort	404	Canada Nettle	308
Bryony, White	72	" Root	339
" Wild	72	" Tea	115
Buchu	74	Canadian Bur	231
" Long	73	Cancer Drops	89
Buckbean	75	" Root	89
Buckthorn Brake	76	" Weed	90
Buckthorn	77	Candle Berry	43
" European	78	Cane, Sweet	432
" Purging	77	Canella	91
" Alder	78	Canker Lettuce	92
Bucku	74	" Root	93, 288, 206
Bugbane	133	" Violet	90
Bugle, Bitter	79	" Weed	93
" Sweet	80	Canoe Wood	456
" Water	80	Caraway	94
" Weed	80	Cardamom	95
Buglewort	80	Cardinal, Blue	96
Bugloss	67	" Flower	97
Bugwort	133	" Red	97
Buku	74	Cardus, Spotted	98
Bullock's Eye	232	Carolina Jessamine	251
Bullsfoot	141	Carpenter's Herb	80
Burdock	81	" Square	384
" Sea	127	Carragheen	244
Bur Marigold	153	Carrion Flower	247
Burning Bush	82, 453	Carrot, Wild	99
Burrage	67	Cascarilla	102
Bur-reed, Spiny	83	Cassia	103

Cassia Fistula	104	Chillies	327
Cascara Amarga	100	Chilly Pepper	327
" Sagrada	101	China Root	467
Castor Oil Plant	318	" Root, American	121
Catarrh Root	197	Chink	115
Catch Fly	56	Chirayta	122
" Weed	126	Chiretta	122
Catmint	105	Chittam Bark	101
Catnip	105	Chocolate, Indian	32
Catsfoot	247, 397	" Root	32
Cat's-paw	247	Cicily, Sweet	123
Catswort	105	Cicuta	124
Cedar Apples	106	Cinnamon, White	91
" Red	106	" Wild	91
" White	22	" Wood	378
Celandine, Garden	107	Cinquefoil	189
" Wild	108	Citronelle	37
Celery	109	Clabbergrass	126
Centaury, American	110	Clammy Sage	125
" Ground	111	Clapwort	89
" Red	110	Clary	125
Century Plant, Am	9	Clary, Wild	125
Cereus, Night-blooming	87	Clear Eye	125
Chafe Weed	267	Cleaver Grass	128
Chamomile	112	Cleavers	126
" Garden	113	Cleaverwort	126
" German	114	Clivers	126
" Low	113	Clotbur	81, 127
" Roman	112	Cloud Berry Root	59
" Spanish	324	Clove Garlic	199
" Wild	291	" Pepper	334
Chamomilla	114	Clover, Broom	243
Checkerberry	115	" Red	128
Cheese Rennet Herb	126	" Sweet	256
Cheeses	281	" White	129
Cherry, Black	116	Cloves	130
" Poison, Black	49	Coakum	198
" Wild	116	Coca Leaves	131
Chervil, Sweet	123	Cocash Root	132
Chestnut	117	" Weed	268
" Horse	118	Cockleburr	11
Chickweed	119	Cockscomb, Red	333
" Red	393	Cockspur, Rye	173
Chicory	120	Cock up-hat	353
Chiendent	255	Cocowort	392
Children's Bane	124	Cohosh, Black	133

Cohosh, Blue	134	Cramp Bark	149
" Red	135	Cranberry, High	149
" White	136	" Mountain	446
Colchicum	137	Cranesbill	150
Cold Seeds	350, 455	Crawley Root	151
Cold Water Root	132	Creeper, Virginia	246
Colic Root	61, 467	Crosswort	66
Coliander Seeds	145	Crow Corn Root	61
Collard	86	Crowfoot	150
Colocynth	138	" Acrid	84
Colomba Root	140	Crystalwort	274
Colombo	140	Cubebs	152
" American	139	Cuckold	153
Columbo	140	Cuckoo Bread	391, 409
Columbo Root	140	" Pint	242
Coltsfoot	141	Cucumber, Bitter	138
Colt's-tail	191	Cud Weed	267, 299
Columbrina	311	Culver's Physic	60
Comb Flower	430	" Root	60
Comfrey	142	Cummin Seed	154
Compass Plant Weed	366	" " Black	154
Condor Vine	155	" " Sweet	154
Cone Disk	435	Cundurango	155
Cone Flower	435	Cup Plant, Indian	237
Consumption Brake	143	Curcuma	443
Consumption Weed	92	" Ohio	205
Consumptives' Weed	470	Cureall	32, 37
Convulsion Weed	188	Cusso	156
Coolwort	144		
Coral Root	151	Daisy, Ox-eye	157
Coriander	145	" White	157
Cornel, Florida	69	Damiana Flowers	158
Cornel, Round-leaved	316	Damson, Mountain	351
Corpse Plant	188	Dandelion	159
Cossoo	156	Dead Mens Bells	193
Costmary	146	Dead Nettle	18
Cotton Plant Root	147	Death of Man	124
Couch Grass	255	Deer Berry	115, 419
Cough Root	51	" Tongue	160
" Weed	268	Devil's Bit	396
Countryman's Treacle	367	" Bones	467
Cowbane, Spotted	124	Dielytra	442
Cow Cabbage	270	Dillisk	166
Cowhage	148	Dill Seed	161
" Plant Seed, The	148	Dillydil Weed	291
Cow Lily	271	Dittany	162

G. S. CHENEY CO.

Dittany, American...	162	Elder Prickly........	169
" Mountain....	162	" South'n Prickly	169
Dock, Curled........	164	" Sweet.........	167
" Narrow	164	" Wild..........	168
" Water........	163	Elecampane........	170
" Great Water..	163	Eleuthera Bark.....	102
" Yellow........	164	Elk Wood..........	171
Dogachamus.........	316	Elm, Indian........	172
Dog Button	311	" Red..........	172
" Fennel.........	291	" Slippery......	172
" Grass..........	255	" Sweet.........	172
" Rose...........	165	Emetic Herb........	275
" Tree...........	69	" Root........	417
" Weed..........	255	" Weed.......	275
Dogsbane...........	56	Englishman's Foot..	338
Dog's Finger........	193	Ergot........	173
Dogwood, Alder-leaved	316	Eryngo, Water......	174
" Black.....	78	Euphorbia..........	175
" Broad-leaved	316	Evans Root........	32
" Florida....	69	Eve's Cup..........	454
" Swamp....	317	Eye Balm..........	205
" Virginia..	69	" Root..........	205
Donkeys' Eyes......	148	Eyebright.... ......110, 275	
Door Weed........216, 329			
Dragon Root........	242	Fairy Fingers.......	193
Dragon's Claw......	151	" Gloves........	193
Dragonwort.........	55	False Coltsfoot......	397
Dropberry..........	405	" Grapes........	246
Dropsy Plant.......	37	Featherfew.........	182
Duckretter..........	220	Febrifuge Plant....	182
Duck's Foot........	283	Felonwort..........	58
Dulse..............	166	Felwort............	200
Dwale..............	49	Female Fern........ 33, 341	
Dwarf Ground Nut..	203	" Regulator ..	268
" Mallow........	281	Fennel Seed	176
Dysentery Weed....	299	Fenugreek..........	177
		Fern Bush..........	180
Eagle Vine.........	155	Fern Gale..........	179
Earth Gall..........	220	" Male.......... 76, 178	
Earth Smoke.......	196	" " Shield....	178
Easter Giant	55	" Meadow.......	179
East India Catarrh		" Rattlesnake.....	143
Root	197	" Rock...........	280
Elder......	167	" Root..........	341
" Common,......	167	" Royal Flowering	76
" Dwarf.........	168	" Spleen	180

BOTANIC DRUGGISTS.

Fern Spleenwort....	180
" Sweet.........	180
Ferry, Sweet.......	180
Feverfew...........	182
Fever Bush........	181
" Root..........151, 183	
" Tree......... 184, 192	
" Tree of Australia	184
" Twig.........	57
" Twitch......	57
" Wood........	181
Feverwort..........	66
Fieldwort...........	291
Field Balsam........	267
" Weed........	291
Figwort............185, 384	
" Herb........	384
" Knotty-rooted	185
" Water......	54
Finger Flower......	193
" Leaf.........	189
Fir Tree............	186
Fire Weed.........	187
Firrape	89
Fish-mouth.........	38
Fit Plant...........	188
" Root............	188
Fivefinger.........	189
Fivefingers Root....	203
Five Leaves........	246
Flag Lily...........	04
" Sweet..........	432
Flagroot, Blue......	64
" Sweet.....	432
Flannel Flower......	302
Flax, Mountain......	400
Flaxseed.......	190
Fleabane............	191
" Canada....	191
" Philadelphia	382
Flesh colored Asclepias	240
Florida Bark........	192
" Bean........	148
Flower de luce......	64
Flux Root........ ..	339
Flytrap............. 56, 454	
Foles Foot..........	141
Folks' Glove.........	193
Forefathers' Cup..	454
Foxglove...........	193
" Purple....	193
Friar's Cap.........	3
" Cowl........	3
Fringe Tree........	194
" " False...	1
Frog Lily....... ..	271
Frost Plant.........	195
" Weed........	195
Frostwort....	195
Fucus..............	387
Fullers' Herb......	404
Fumitory...........	196
Fustic, Young......	1
Gag Root...........	275
Galangal............	197
Galangale..	197
Galangall...........	197
Gale, Sweet.........	179
Galls..............	309
Garantogen........ ...	203
Garget.....	198
Garlic........	199
Gayfeather..........	396
Gem Fruit	144
Gentian	200
" American ..	201
" Blue....	201
" Yellow.........	139
Georgia Bark........	192
Geranium, Spotted..	150
Germander	373
Gill-over-the-ground.	247
Gillrun.............	247
Ginger, African.....	202
" Indian	397
" Jamaica....	202
" Wild	397
Ginseng...........	203
" Blue	134
" Yellow ...,..	134
Gypsywort..........	80

Goatsbane	3	Hellebore, American	220
Golden bough	296	" Black	217
Golden Motherwort	267	" False	7, 220
Golden Rod	204	" Fetid	86, 218
" " Sweet scented	204	" Green	220
		" Stinking	218
Goldenseal	205	" " Black	218
Golden Senecio	268	" Swamp	220
Goldthread	206	" White	219
Goosefoot	313	" " Am.	220
Goose-grass	126	" " European	219
Goose's Hare	126		
Grains Paradise	207	Helmet Flower	385
Gravel Plant	208	" Pod	444
Gravel Root	352	Hemlock	221
" Weed	208	" American	124
Grindelia	209	" " Water	124
Ground Apple	113	" Poison	124
" Berry	115	" Spotted	124, 125
" Holly	337	" Water	124
" Laurel	208	" Wild	124, 125
" Lily	51	Hemp, Black Indian	239
" Lemon	283	" White "	240
" Moss	212	Henbane	222
Guaiac Wood	210	Herb Christopher	76
Guarana	211	Hickory Tree	390
Guinea Grains	207	Highbelia	96
Gum Plant	142	Hig Taper	302
Gunbright	368	Hillberry	115
		Hindheel	434
		Hini	60
Hackmatac	433	Hippo	417
Hair-cap Moss	212	" Indian	241
Hardhack	213, 422	Hip Tree	165
Hardock	81	Hive Vine	419
Hareburr	81	Hog Apple	283
Hares Beard	302	" Bean	222
Hartshorn Bush	76	Hogweed	466
Harvest Lice	153	Holly American	223
Haw, Black	214	Holly Sea	224
Hawkweed	63	Hollyhock	225
Haymaids	247	Holmes' Weed	384
Healall	215, 384, 422	Holy Herb	470
Healing Herb	142	Honey Bloom	56
Heartsease	216	Honeysuckle, Bush	226
Hedgemaids	247	Hoodwort	385

BOTANIC DRUGGISTS.

Hops	227	Indigo Weed	243
" Wild	72	" Wild	243
Hop Tree	347	" Wild, False	243
Horehound	228	" Yellow	243
" Water	80	Ink Root	288
" White	228	Ipecac, American	175
Horse Balm	422	" Milk	417
" Flea Weed	243	" White	175
" Fly Weed	243	" Wild	175, 183
" Gentian	183	Irish Moss	244
Horse-heal	170	Iron Wood	245
Horse Hoof	141	Itch Weed	220
" Mint	294	Ivory Plum	115
" " Sweet	162	Ivy	261
" Pipe	368	" Bark, American	246
" Radish	229	" Big-leaved	260
Horse-tail Rush	368	" Ground	247
Horse Weed	191, 213, 230, 422	" Poison	340
Hound's Tongue	231		
House Leek	232	Jaborandi	248
" " Small	233	Jack-in-the pulpit	242
Hove	247	Jacob's Ladder	2, 249
Huckleberry	457	Jalap	250
Huntsman's Cup	454	" Cancer	198
Hurr-burr	81	" Wild	284
Hydrangea	234	Jamestown Weed	437
" Wild	234	Jaundice Berry	40
Hyeble	168	" Root	205
Hyssop	235	Jerusalem Tea	313
" Wild	448	Jessamine, Yellow	251
		Jesuit's Bark	331
Iceland Moss	236	Jewel Weed	168
Ice Plant	188	Jew'sharp Plant	51
" Vine	319	Jimson Weed	437
Indian Cup	237	Job's Tears	252
" Dream	363	Joepye	352
" Hemp, Am	238	Johnswort	253
" Lettuce	139	Juniper Berries	254
" Paint	62	" Bush	254
" Pipe	188		
" Plant	205		
" Physic	241	Kassamah Root	197
" Posey	267	Kidney Root	352
" Root	413	King's Clover	256
" Shoe	297	" Cure	337
" Turnip	242	" Fern	76

Kinnikinnick	316, 446	Lettuce Garden	265
Kino Root, American	150	" Liverwort	92
Knight's Spur	259	" White	93
Knitback	142	" Wild	92, 266
Knob Grass	422	Licorice	273
" Root	433	Life Everlasting	267
Knot Grass	255	Life-of-man	413
" Weed, Spotted	216	Life Root	268
Knotty Brake	178	Lignum Vitæ	210
Kola	257	Lily, Pond	270
Koosso	156	" White	270
Kousso	156	" White Pond	270
Kussander	284	" Yellow	271
		Lime Tree	42, 272
Labrador Tea	258	" " Fruit	5
Ladies' Glove	193	Linden	42
" Slipper	297	" Flowers	272
" Thumb	216	Linseed	190
Lad's Love	410	Lion's Ear	298
Lake Weed	329	" Foot	93
Lambkill	261	" Tail	298
Lambs' Quarter	51	" Tooth	159
Larch	433	Lily of the Valley	269
" American	433	Liver Leaf	274
" Black	433	" " Kidney	274
Lark Heel	259	" Lily	64
Lark's Claw	259	" Moss	274
Larkspur	259	" Weed	274
Laurel	44	Liverwort	274
" American	260	" Noble	274
" Broad-leaved	260	Lobelia	275
" Mountain	260	" Blue	96
" Narrow-leaved	261	" Red	97
" Poison	261	Locust Bloom	272
" Sheep	261	" Plant	388
Lavender	262	Lofty Quassia	351
" Garden	262	Loose Strife	460
" Thrift	288	Lords and Ladies	242
Lavose	276	Lovage	276
Leaf Cup, Yellow	46	Love lies bleeding	333
Leather Bush	263	Lungwort	277
Leatherwood	263	" Bullock's	302
Leaver Wood	263	" Maple	278
Leopardsbane	24	Lupuline	227
Leptandra, Purple	60	Lyre Tree	456
Lettuce, Acrid	264		

Mace	310	Milk Sweet	126
Mad Apple	437	Milkweed	293, 417
Mad-dog-weed	385	" Common	293
Madweed	385	" Wandering	56
Magnolia	279	Mistletoe	296
Maidenhair	280	Mitrewort	144
Mallow, Low	281	Moccasin Root	297
" Marsh	282	Mohawk Weed	50
Mandrake	283	Monkey Flower	297
" American	283	Monkshood	3
Man-in-the-ground	284	Moon Flower	75
Man-of-the-earth	284	Moonseed	320
Man Root	284	Moosewood	263
Maple, Ground	374	Mortification Root	282
" Red	285	Motherwort	298
" Swamp	285	Mountain Box	446
Marcory	353	" Mint	35, 295
Marestail	458	" Sweet	358
Marjoram, Sweet	287	Mourning Bride	382
Marsh, Clover	75	" Widow	382
" Rosemary	288	Mousebane	3
" Turnip	242	Mouse Ear	299
Marigold	286	Mouth Root	206
Mary Bud	286	" Smart	70
Masterwort	18, 289	Mugwort	300
Matico Plant	290	Mulberry	301
Maudlin, Water	12	Mullein	302
Maudlinwort	157	Musk Root	427
May Flower	208	Musquash Root	124
" Queen Moss	212	Mustard, Black	303
" Weed	291	" White	304
Maywort	291	Myrrh	305
Meadow Bloom	84	Myrtle	43
" Cabbage	86	" Bog	75
" Pride	139	" Dutch	179
" Root	288	" Flag	432
" Scabish	132	" Grass	432
" Sweet	213, 241	" Sweet	432
Meal Berry	446	" Wax	43
Mealy Tree	25		
Mechameck	284	Naked Ladies	137
Mechoacan	284	Nanny Berry	306
Melilot	256	" Bush	306
Mezereon	292	Necklace Weed	136
" American	263	Neckweed	70, 238
Milfoil	468		

Nephritic Plant	307	Ozier, Green	316
Nerve Root	297	" Red	317
Nest Root	188		
Nettle	308	Palma Christi	318
Networt	398	Pappoose Root	134
New Jersey Tea	358	Paradise Seed	207
Nightshade, Deadly	49	Pareira Brava	319
" Fetid	222	Parilla, Yellow	320
" Garden	58	Pariswort	51
" Stinking	222	Parsley	321
" Woody	58	" Poison	124
Ninsin	203	" Sea	276
Noah's Ark	297	" Water	124
Noble Pine	337	Parsnip, Cow	289
Nosebleed	468	Partridge Berry	115, 419
Nutgalls	309	Passion Flower	322
Nutmegs	310	Pasque Flower	349
Nux Metella	311	Patience Dock	55
" Vomica	311	Paul's Betony	80
		Peach	323
		Peachwort	216
Oak Bark, Black	312	Pearl Moss	244
" " Red	312	Pelican Flower	401
" " White	312	Pellitory Bark	28
Oak, Dyers'	309	" Bastard	402
" of Jerusalem	313	" German	402
" Poison	340	" of Spain	324
Oil Nut	85	" Root	324
Old Maid's Pink	404	Pennyroyal	325
Old Man	410	Peony	326
Olive, Spurge	292	Pepper, Bird	327
One Berry	419	" Black	328
Onion, Bog	242	" Bush, Sweet	16
" Sea	420	" Cayenne	327
Orange Flowers	314	" Elder	290
" Peel	314	" Jamaica	334
" Root	205	" Java	152
" " Climbing	57	" Maleguetta	207
Orcanette	17	" Red	327
Orris Root	315	" Water	329
Osier, Green	316	Pepperidge Bush	40
" Red	317	Peppermint	330
Oswego Tea	35	Peruvian Bark	331
Ova-ova	188	Persian Berries	78
Oxadoddy	60	Petty Morrel	413
Ox Balm	422	Pewterwort	368

Physic, Indian	241	Polypod Rock	341
" Root	60	Polypody	341
Picac	417	Pomegranate	342
Pichi	332	" Fruit	342
Pickaway Anise	347	Pompion	350
Pickerel Weed	394	Pool Root	376
Pickpocket	392	Poolwort	376
Pickpurse	392	Poor Man's Pharmacetty	392
Pigeon Berry	198	Poor Robin	126
" Tree	169	Poplar, American	343
Pilewort	333	" Balsam	36
Pilot Weed	366	" Bark	343
Pimento	334	" Carolina	36
Pimpernel, Blue	385	" Tacamahac	36
" Scarlet	393	" White	343, 456
" Small	381	" Wild	456
" Water	70	" Yellow	456
Pine, White	335	Poppy	344
" Tulip	297, 337	Potato, Wild	284
Pink, Carolina	336	Poverty Weed	267
" Indian	336	Prairie Bush, Stinking	347
" Mountain	208	" Dock	345
" Root	336	" Grub	347
" Winter	208	" Pine	396
Pipsissewa	337	" Weed	345
" Spotted	462	Prickly Pear	87
Pistachio	464	Prickwood	82
Pitcher Plant	454	Pride of China	45
Plantain	338	" of India	45
" Net leaf	398	Pride Weed	191
" Spotted	398	Priest's Crown	159
Pleurisy Root	339	" Pintle	242
Pock Wood,	210	Prim	346
Poison Berry	135	Primrose, Evening	383
" Flag	64	" Tree	383
" Nut	311	Primwort	346
" Tobacco	222	Princes' Feather	333
" Vine	340	" Pine	337
Poke	198	Privet	346
" Indian	220	Privy	346
" Stinking	86	Ptelea	347
" Virginia	198	Puccoon, Red	62
" Weed	198	" Yellow	205
Polar Plant	366	Puff-ball	159
Polecat Weed	86	Puke Weed	275
Pollom, Red	115	Pulsatilla	349

Pumpkin Seed	350	Rattlesnake Root.	51, 93, 133
Punic Apple	342	" Weed	63, 174
Punk	440	Ratsbane	311
Purging Berries	77	Red Berry	203
" Root	417	" " Tea	115
Purple Cone Flower	348	" Gum	357
Purslain, Milk	417	" Ink Plant	198
" White	417	" Rod	317
Pursley, Milk	417	" Root	358
" White	417	" Seed	445
Purvain	448	" Shanks	216
Pyramid Flower	139	" Weed	198
" Plant	139	" Wood	379
Pyrola	337	Rhatany	359
" Round-leaved	92	Rheumatism Root	444
		Rhubarb, American	361
Quack Grass	255	" India	362
Quaker Button	311	Rhus Aromatica	360
Quassia	351	Richweed	133, 422
Queen's Delight	353	Robin-run-away	247
Queen of the Meadow	352	Robin-run-in-the-hedge	147
Queen's Root	353	Rock Rose	195
Querbraco	354	Rope Bark	263
Quickens	255	Rose, Christmas	217
Quick-in-the-hand	108	" Dog	165
Quick Grass	255.	" Pink	110
Quillai Bark	403	" Flowers, Pale	364
Quillaya	403	" " Red	364
Quince Seed	355	Rosemary Leaves	365
Quitch	255	Rosey Bush	213
" Grass	255	Rosin Weed	237, 366
Quitel	60	Rough Root	396
Quiver Leaf	343	Round-leaved Plantain	338
		" " Sundew	429
Rabbits' Root	377	Round Wood	27
Raccoon Berry	283	Rue	367
Ragged Cup	237	Rush, Dutch	368
Ragweed	466	" Polishing	368
Ragwort	268	" Scouring	368
Rainbow Weed	460	" Sweet	432
Raspberry	356	Rye, Robins'	212
" Ground	205	" Smut of	173
" Red	356	" Spurred	173, 369
Rattle-Bush	243	" Cockspur	173
Rattle Root	133		
Rattlesnake Leaf	398	Sabadilla	370

Sacred Bark	101	Scarlet Berry	58
Saffron	371	Scammony, Wild	284
" American	371	Scratch Weed	126
" Bastard	371	Scrofula Plant	384
" Dyers'	371	Scrubby Grass	386
Saffron False	371	Scullcap	385
" Meadow	137	" Blue	385
Sagackhomi	446	Scullcap-Side-flowering	385
Sage	372	Scurvy Grass	386
" Indian	66	Sea Beans	148
" Lyre-leaved	90	" Holly	224
" Meadow	90	" Lavender	288
" Wild	90	Seal Root	405
" Wood	373	Sealwort	405
St. Christopher Herb	76	Sea Wrack	387
" Johnswort	253	Sedge, Sweet	432
Salad	265	Seneca Root	400
Saloop	378	Senega "	400
Salt Rheum Weed	38	Senna, Alexandrian	389
" Rock Moss	244	" American	388
Sangree Root	401	" India	389
Sangrel	401	' Wild	388
Sanicle, American	374	Septfoil	439
" Black	375	Setwall	447
" White	376	Seven Barks	234
Sarsaparilla, American	377	Shag-bark Tree	390
" Bristlestem	168	" Walnut	390
" False	377	Shamrock	391
" Spanish	377	" Indian	51
" Texas	320	" Water	75
" Wild	377	Sheep Berry	306
" Yellow	320	" Poison	261
Sassafras	378	" Weed	404
" Swamp	279	Shell-flower	38
Saunders, Red	379	Shepherds' Club	302
Savin	380	" Knot	439
Savoyan	126	" Purse	392
Sawwort	396	" Weather-glass	393
Saxifrage	381	Shield Root	178
" Small	381	Shin Leaf	92
" " Burnet	381	Shot Bush	169
Saxifrax	378	Shovel Weed	394
Scabious	191	Shrub Yellow Root	469
" Sweet	382	Sicily Root	123
Scabish	383	Sickle Weed	329
Scabwort	170		

Side-saddle Flower..	454	Snakeweed Poison ..	124
" Plant...	454	Snapping Hazel.....	464
Silkweed............	293	Snap Weed.........	108
" Common...	293	Snapwood	181
" Rose-colored	240	Sneezewort..........402,	431
Silky Cornel........	317	Snowball, Wild.....	358
Silver Leaf..........	213	Soap Tree Bark.....	403
Silver Weed........	213	Soapwort...........	404
Simpler's Joy........	448	Soldiers' Herb......	290
Skevish............	382	Solomon Seal.......	405
Skoke	198	" Giant..	405
Skunk Weed........	86	" Small..	407
Sleepwort...........	265	Sorrel, Mountain....	408
Slipper Root........	297	" Sheep.......	409
Slippers............	108	" Tree........	171
Sloe	214	" Wood........391,	409
Sloven Wood.......	410	Sour Trefoil	391
Smallpox Plant......	454	Sourwood..........	406
Smart Weed........	329	Southernwood.......	410
Smellage............	276	Spadic.............	131
Smilax, Boston......	395	Spanish Juice.......	273
" Cape........	395	" Needles....	153
Smoke Plant........	1	" Pepper	327
" Tree	1	Sparrow Grass......	31
Snake Bite.......... 51,	266	Spatter Dock.......	271
" Head.........	38	Spearmint	411
" Leaf, Yellow..	6	Speedwell....	412
" Lily	64	" Tall	60
" Milk.........	417	" Virginia ..	412
Snakeroot, Black.....133,	375	Spice Berry........	115
" Button.. 174,	396	" Birch	53
" Canada...	397	" Bush.........	181
" Coltsfoot.	397	" Fever Bush..	181
" Corn.....	174	" Wood	181
" Heart....	397	Spignet.............	413
" Rattle ...133,	398	Spikenard	413
" Red Berry	135	" American	413
" Sampson.	399	" Small ...	377
" Senaga..	400	" Tree.....	169
" Seneka..	400	Spindle Tree........	82
" Southern.	397	Spleen Amaranth...	333
" Vermont.	397	Spleenwort..........	414
" Virginia .	401	" Bush.....	180
" White....	376	Spoonhunt..........	260
" " Berry	136	Spoonwort..........	386
Snakeweed......266, 384.	401	Spotted Comfrey....	277

Spotted Lungwort...	277	Strawberry Shrub...	82
Spruce, Hemlock....	221	Strophanthus.	424
" Weeping ...	221	Succory............	120
Spunk	415	" Wild.......	120
Spurge............	175	Sumach............	426
" Black........	416	" Climbing....	340
" Blooming....	417	" Pennsylvania	426
" Large Flow'ing	417	" Smooth.....	426
" Spotted......	416	" Upland......	426
" Large Spotted	418	Sumbul	427
Square Stalk........	384	Summer Savory.....	428
Squaw Bush........	149	Sundew............	429
" Mint.......	325	Sundrops...........	383
" Root........	133	Sunflower	430
" Vine........	419	" False	431
" Weed	268	" Garden....	430
Squill..............	420	" Swamp....	431
Squirrel Pea, Ground	444	Sutterberry.........	28
Staff Tree, Climbing.	57	Swallowwort	293
Staff-vine...........	57	" Orange..	339
Stagger-weed........	442	" Silky....	293
Stammerwort........	466	Swamp Cabbage....	86
Star Bloom	336	" Milkweed...	240
Starchwort..........	242	Swan Weed........	132
Star Flower........	132	Sweating Plant......	66
" Grass...........	61	Sweat Root........	2
" " False	61	" Weed.........	282
" Root...........	61	Sweet Bush.........	180
Starwort, Drooping...	445	" Gum Bark....	423
Stave Wood.........	351	" Liquorice.....	273
Steeple Bush	213	" Lucerne.......	256
Stick Seed..........	153	" Magnolia....	279
Stickwort...........	11, 437	" Root	432
Stillingia...........	353	Sweet-scented Life	
Stinging Nettle.......	308	Everlasting........	267
Stinking Chamomile.	291	Sweet-scented Water	
" Weed.......	313	Lily..............	270
Stinkwort	437	Sweet-smelling Trefoil	12
Stitchwort..........	119	Sweet Viburnum....	306
Stone Brake........	341	" Willow	179
" Mint	162	" Wood	273
" Root	422	" " Bark ..	102
Storax Bark........	423	Swine Snout........	159
Stork's Bill.........	150		
Strawberry	425	Tailed Pepper......	152
" Bush.......	82	Tallow, Bayberry....	43

Tallow, Shrub.	43	Touch Wood	440
" Vegetable, Am.	43	Toywort	392
Tamarack	433	Trailing Sumach	340
Tansy	434	Traveller's Joy,	448
" Double	434	Tree Lungwort	278
" Double-flowered	434	Trefoil	274
Tea Berry	115	" Marsh	75
" Mountain	115	" Shrubby	347
Tearel	66	Tree of Heaven	441
Tetter Berry	72	Trembling Poplar	343
Tetterwort	107	" Tree	343
Thick Weed	325	Trillium	51
Thimbleweed	435	Truelove	51
Thistle, Bitter	98	Trumpet Weed	352
" Canada	436	Tuber Root	339
" Cursed	436	Tulip Poplar	456
" Holy	98, 436	" Tree	456
" Root	436	Tun Hoof	247
Thorn-apple	437	Turkey Claw	151
Thoroughstem	66	" Corn	442
Thorough Wax	66	" Pea	442
Thoroughwort	66	Tumeric Root	443
Three-leaved Arum	242	Turnip, Dragon	242
Thrift, American	288	" Indian	242
Throat Root	32	" Meadow	242
Throatwort	396	" Pepper	242
Throwwort	298	" Swamp	242
Thunder Plant	232	" Wild	242
Thyme	438	Turpentine Sunflower	345
" Basil	88	Turtle-bloom	38
Tickle Weed	220	Turtle-head	38
Tick Weed	325	Twin-leaf	444
Tilia Flowers	272		
Tinker's Weed	183	Umbel	297
Toad Lily	270	Uncum	268
" Root	135	Unicorn	61, 445
Tobacco, Indian	275	" False	445
" Mountain	24	" Root,	61
" Wild	275	Unicorns' Horn	445
" Wood	464	Universe Vine	446
Toothache Bush	28	Upland Cranberry	446
" Tree	28	Uvadalia	46
Tormentil, American	150	Uva Ursi	446
Tormentilla	439		
Tory Weed	231	Valerian, American	297
Touch-me-not	108	" Am. English	447

Valerian Am. Greek	2	White Beads	136
" False	268	" Cap	213
" English	447	" Leaf	213
" Officinal	447	" Root	339
Vandal Root	447	" Weed	456
Vanilla Leaf	160	" Wood	157
Velvet Leaf	319	Whorlywort	60
Velvet Plant	302	Whortleberry	457
Venus' Cup	297	" Black.	457
" Shoe	297	Wickup	458
Vervain	448	Wicopy Herb	458
" American	448	" Indian	458
" Blue	448	Wig Tree	1
" False	448	Wild Allspice	181
Violet, Adder's	398	" Brier	165
" Birdsfoot	449	" Coffee	183
" Bloom	58	" Jessamine	251
" Blue	449	" Lemon	283
" Canker	450	" Licorice	377
" Dogstooth	6	" Mandrake	283
Vine Maple	320	' Rhubarb	284
Virginia Cowslip	277	" Woodvine	246
" Stone Crop	451	Willow Herb	458
Virgin's-bower	452	" " Hooded	385
Vomitwort	275	" " Purple	460
		" Pussy	459
Wafer Ash	347	" Red	317
Wahoo	453	" Rose	317
Wake Robin	242	" Sage	460
Wallflower, Western	56	" White	461
Walnut	390	Wind Root	339
" Lemon	85	Wing Seed	347
" White	85	Winter Berry	13
Water Cabbage	270	" Bloom	404
" Cup	454	" Clover	419
" Flag	64	" Fern	363
" Nerve Root	240	Wintergreen	337
Watermelon	455	" Pear Leaf	92
Waw Weed	268	" Round-Leaved	92
Wax Berry	43	Wintergreen, Spicy	115
" Cluster	115	" Spotted	462
Waxwork	57	" Spring	115
Waythorn	77	Winter's Bark	463
Weathercock	108	Witch Grass	255
Whistle Wood	285	" Hazel	464
White Bay	279		

Wolf Foot	80	Yam Root, Wild	467
" Grape	58	Yarrow	468
" Root	3	Yaw Root	353
Wolfsbane	24, 3	Yellow Berry	283
Woodbine	246, 456, 251	" Eye	205
Woody Climber	246	" Ladies' Slipper	297
Woolen	302	" Lily Root	271
Woolybut	184	" Moccasin	297
Worm Grass	336	" Paint Root	205
" Root, American	336	" Root	57, 205, 206, 469
Wormseed	313	" Umbel	297
" American	313	" Wood	28
Wormwood	465	Yerba Santa	470
" Roman	466	Youthwort	429
Wymote	282		

BOTANICAL INDEX.

** The numbers refer to the paragraph not the page.

Abies balsamea.	186	Anacyclus Pyrethrum	324
" Canadensis	221	Anagallis arvensis	393
Acer rubrum	285	Anchusa tinctoria	17
Achillea Millefolium	468	Andromeda arborea	171
" Ptarmica	402	Anemone Pulsatilla	349
Aconitum Napellus	3	Anethum graveolens	161
Acorus Calamus	432	Angelica atropurpurea	18
Actæa alba	136	Anthemis Cotula	291
" rubra	135	" nobilis	112, 113
Adiantum pedatum	280	Apium graveolens	109
Adonis Vernolis	7	Aplectrum hyemale	4
Æsculus Hippocastanum	118	Apocynum androsæmifolium	56
Agathotes Chirayta	122	Apocynum cannabinum	239
Agave Americana	9	Aralia hispida	168
" Virginica	10	" nudicaulis	377
Agrimonia Eupatoria	11	" racemosa	413
Ailanthus Glandulosus	441	" spinosa	169
Aletris farinosa	61	Arctium lappa	81
Allium sativum	199	Arctostaphylos Uva Ursi	446
Alnus rubra	14	Areca Catechu	23
" serrulata	15	Aristolochia Serpentaria	401
Alpina Galanga	197	Arnica Montana	24
Althæa officinalis	282	Artanthe elongata	290
" rosea	225	Artemisia abrotanum	410
Amarantus hypochondriacus	333	" Absinthium	465
Ambrosia artemisiæfolia	466	" vulgaris	300
" trifida	230	Arisæmar triphyllum	242
Amomum Granum paradisi	207	Asarum Canadense	397
Amomum Zingiber	202	Asclepias cornuti	293
Ampelopsis quinquefolia	246	" incarnata	240
Amygdalus Persica	323	" mataperro	155
		" Syriaca	293
		" tuberosa	339

Asparagus officinalis.	31	Castanea Americana.	117
Aspidium Filix Fœmina	33	Caulophyllum thalictroides	134
Aspidium Filix Mas..	178		
Aspidosperma Quebracho	354	Ceanothus Americana	358
		Celastrus scandens..	57
Asplenium Adiantum	314	Centaurea benedicta	98
Aster puniceus	132	Cetraria Islandica..	236
Atropa Belladonna..	49	Chelidonium majus...	107
		Chelone glabra	38
Balsamodendron Myrrha	305	Chenopodium Botrys	313
Baptisia tinctoria	243	Chimaphila maculata	462
Barosma Serratifolia	73	" umbellata	337
" crenata	74	Chionanthus Virginica	194
Berberis vulgaris	40	Chondrus crispus	244
Betonica officinalis..	52	Cichorium intybus	120
Betula lenta	53	Cimicifuga racemosa	133
Bidens frondosa	153	Cinchona Calisaya	331
" tripartita	48	Cirsium arvensis	436
Boletus fomentarius..	415	Cissampelos Pareira.	319
" ignarius	8	Citrullus colocynthis.	138
" laricis	8	Citrus Aurantium	314
Borago officinalis	67	" Limetta	5
Botrychium fumaroides	143	Clematis Virginica	452
Brayera anthelmintica	156	Clethra alnifolia	16
Bryonia alba	72	Cocculus palmatus..	140
Buxus sempervirens..	68	Cochlearia officinalis.	386
		Coix lachryma	252
Cactus grandiflorus...	87	Cola Acuminata	257
" Opuntia	87	Colchicum autumnale	137
Calamintha officinalis	88	Collinsonia Canadensis	422
Calendula "	286	Comptonia asplenifolia	180
Canella alba	91	Conium maculata	124
Cannabis Indica	238	Convallaria Majalis..	269
" sativa	238	" multiflora	405
Capsella bursa-pastoris	392	" racemosa	407
Capsicum annuum	327	Convolvulus panduratus	284
" baccatum.	327	Coptis trifolia	206
Carthamus tinctorius	371	Corallorhiza odontorhiza	151
Carum carui	94	Coriandrum sativum.	145
Carya alba	390	Cornus Circinata	316
Caryophyllus aromaticus	130	" Florida	69
Cassia acutifolia	389	" sericea	317
" cinnamonium.	103	Corydalis formosa	442
" elongata	389	Croton Eleuteria	102
" Fistula	104	Cucurbita Pepo	350
" Marilandica	388	Cuminum Cyminum..	154

Cunila mariana	162	Euphorbia hypericifolia	418
Curcuma longa	443	" Ipecacuanha	175
Cydonia vulgaris	355	" maculata	416
Cynoglossum officinale	231	Euryangium Sumbul	427
Cypripedium pubescens	297		
Cytisus Scoparius	71	Fabiana Imbricata	332
		Fagus ferruginea	47
Daphne Mezereum	292	Fœniculum officinale	176
Datura Stramonium	437	Fragaria vesca	425
Daucus Carota	99	" Virginiana	425
Delphinium consolida	259	Frasera Carolinensis	139
" Staphisagria	421	Fraxinus acuminata	30
Diervilla Canadensis	226	" sambucifolia	26
Digitalis purpurea	193	Fucus versiculosus	387
Dioscorea villosa	467	Fumaria officinalis	196
Dirca palustris	263		
Dracocephalum Canariense	39	Galipea officinalis	19
		Galium aparine	126
Drosera rotundifolia	429	Gaultheria procumbens	115
Drymis winteri	463	Gelsemium sempervirens	251
		Gentiana Catesbæi	201
Echinacea angustifolia	348	" lutea	200
Elettaria Cardamomum	95	" ochroleuca	399
Epigæa repens	258	Geranium maculatum	150
Epilobium angustifolium	458	Geum rivale	32
Equisetum hyemale	368	Gillenia trifoliata	241
Erechthites hieracifolius	187	Glycyrrhiza glabra	273
Erigeron Canadense	191	Gnaphalium polycephalum	267
" Philadelphicum	382	Gnaphalium uliginosum	299
Eriodyction Californicum	470	Goodyera pubescens	398
Eriodyction Glutinosum	470	Gossypium herbaceum	147
Eryngium aquaticum	174	Grindelia robusta	209
" ovalifolium	224	Guaiacum officinalis	210
Erythoxylon Coca	131		
Erythronium Americanum	6	Hamamelis Virginica	464
Eucalyptus globulus	184	Hedeoma pulegioides	325
" Rostrata	357	Helenium autumnale	431
Eugenia Pimenta	334	Helianthemum Canadense	195
Euonymus Americana	82	Helianthus annuus	430
" atropurpureus	453	Helleborus fœtidus	218
Eupatorium aromaticum	376	" niger	217
" cannabinum	12	Helonias dioica	445
" perfoliatum	66	Hepatica Triloba	274
" purpureum	352	Heracleum lanatum	289
Euphorbia corollata	417		

Heuchera Americana	374	Lycopus Virginicus..	80
Hieracium venosum.	63	Lythrum salicaria...	460
Humulus Lupulus...	227		
Hydrangea arborescens	234	Magnolia glauca....	279
Hydrastis Canadensis	205	Malva rotundifolia..	281
Hyosciamus niger...	222	Marrubium vulgare..	228
Hypericum perfuratom	253	Matricaria Chamomilla	114
Hyssopus officinalis..	235	Melia Azedarach....	45
		Melilotus officinalis..	256
Ilex opaca..........	223	Melissa Fuchsii.....	34
Impatiens pallida...	108	" officinalis....	37
Inula Helenium.. ..	170	Menispermum Canadense..........	320
Ipomœa Jalapa......	250		
Iris Florentina......	315	Mentha piperita.....	330
" versicolor.......	64	" viridıs......	411
Jeffersonia diphylla..	444	Menyanthes trifoliata	75
Juglans cinerea....	85	Mitchella repens....	419
Juniperus communis.	254	Mitella Nuda........	144
" Sabina....	380	Monarda didyma...	35
" Virginiana	106	" punctata..	294
		Monotropa uniflora..	188
Kalmia angustifolia.	261	Morus rubra........	301
" latifolia.......	260	Mucuna pruriens....	148
Krameria triandria..	359	Myrica cerifera.....	43
		" Gale........	179
Lactuca elongata....	266	Myristica fragrans..	310
" sativa.......	265	Myrsiphyllum asparagoides.........	395
" virosa.......	264		
Larix Americana....	433		
Laurus Benzoin.....	181	Nabalus Albus.....	93
" nobilis......	44	Nasturtium Armorcia	229
Lavandula vera.....	262	Nepeta cataria..	105
Ledum latifolium....	258	" glechoma....	247
Leonurus cardiaca..	298	Nuphar advena.....,	271
Leptandra Virginica.	60	Nymphæa odorata..	270
Leucanthemum vulgare	157		
Liatris odoratissima	160	Ocymum basilicum..	41
" spicata.......	396	Œnothera biennis...	383
Ligusticum levisticum	276	" glauca....	383
Ligustrum vulgare ..	346	Origanum Marjorana	287
Linum usitatissimum	190	Orobanche Virginiana	89
Liquidambar orientale	423	Osmorrhiza longistylis	123
Liriodendron Tulipifera	456	Osmunda regalis....	76
Lobelia cardinalis...	97	Ostrya Virginica....	245
" inflata......	275	Oxalis acetosella....	391
" syphilitica...	96	Oxydendrum arborens	406
Lycopus Europæus..	79	Oxyria reniformis...	408

Pæonia officinalis...	326	Pyrethrum parthenium	182
Panax quinquefolium	203	" tanacetum	146
Papaver somniferum	344	Pyrola rotundifolia..	92
Parthenium integrifolium	307	Pyrus Malus........	21
Passiflora Incarnata	322	Quercus alba........	312
Paullinia sorbilis....	211	" infectoria..	309
Penthorium Sedoides	451	" nigra	312
Petroselinum sativum	321	" rubra.......	312
Peumus Boldus.....	65	Quillaya saponaria..	403
Phytolacca decandra	198		
Picramnia..........	100	Ranunculus acris....	84
Pilocarpus Selloanus	248	Rhamnus catharticus	77
Pimpinella Anisum..	20	" Frangula...	78
" Saxifraga	381	" Purshiana..	101
Pinckneya pubens...	192	Rheum palmatum....	362
Pinus strobus.......	335	" Rhaponticum	361
Piper Cubeba.......	152	Rhodymenia palmata	166
" nigrum.........	328	Rhus Aromatica.....	360
Plantago major......	338	" cotinus........	1
Podophyllum peltatum	283	" glabrum.......	426
Polemonium reptans.	2	" Toxicodendron	340
Polygala Nuttallii....	111	Ricinus communis...	318
" Senega....	400	Rosa canina.........	165
Polygonum Bistorta..	55	" centifolia	364
" hydropiper	329	" Gallica.........	364
" Persicaria	216	Rosmarinus officinalis	365
Polymnia uvedalia...	46	Rubus strigosus	356
Polypodium vulgare..	341	" villosus......	59
Polyporus ignarius....	440	Rudbeckia laciniata..	435
Polytrichum juniperum	212	Rumex acetosella...	409
Populus balsamifera..	36	" aquaticus ...	163
" candicans...	36	" Brittanica ..	163
" tremuloides..	343	" crispus	164
Potentilla Canadensis	189	Ruta graveolens.....	367
" Tormentilla	439		
Prinos verticillatus..	13	Sabbatia angularis.	110
Prunella vulgaris....	215	Salix alba....	461
Prunus Virginiana...	116	" nigra	459
Ptelea trifoliata......	347	Salvia lyrata........	90
Pteris atropurpurea...	363	" officinalis	372
Pterocarpus santalinus	379	" sclarea.......	125
Pulmonaria officinalis	277	Sambucus Canadensis	167
Punica Granatum.....	342	Sanguinaria Canadensis	62
Pycnanthemum montanum	295	Sanicula Marilandica	375
		Saponaria officinalis..	404

Sarracenia purpurea.	454	Tilia Europœa	272
Sassafras Variifolium	378	Trifolium pratense..	128
Satureja hortensis ..	428	" repens	129
Scilla maritima	420	Trigonella Fœnum græ-	
Sclerotium clavus	173, 369	cum	177
Scrophularia aquatica	54	Trillium pendulum..	51
" Marilandica	384	Triosteum perfoliatum	283
" nodosa..	185	Triticum repens	255
Scutellaria lateriflora	385	Turnera aphrodisiaca	158
Secale cornutum	173	Tussilago farfara ...	141
Sedum acre	233		
Sempervivum tectorum	232	Ulmus fulva	172
Senecio aureus	268	Unisema deltifolia..	394
" gracilis	268	Urtica dioica	308
Silphium gummiferum	345	Uvularia grandiflora.	50
" laciniatum.	366	" perfoliata .	50
" perfoliatum	237		
Simaruba excelsa....	351	Vaccinium corymbosum	457
Sinapis alba	304	Valeriana officinalis..	447
" nigra	303	Veratrum album	219
Smilax officinalis	377	" viride	220
" peduncularis.	249	" officinale..	370
" (pseudo) China	121	Verbascum Thapsus	302
Solanum Dulcamara.	58	Verbena hastata	448
Solidago odora	204	Veronica Beccabunga	70
Sorbus Americana..	27	" officinalis...	412
Spigelia Marilandica	336	Viburnum dentatum.	25
Spiræa tomentosa ...	213	" lentago...	306
Statice Caroliniana..	288	" opulus...	149
Stellaria media	119	" prunifolium	214
Sticta pulmonaria ...	278	Viola pedata	449
Stillingia sylvatica..	353	" rostrata	450
Strophanlhus Hispidus	424	Viscum verticillatum	296
Strychnos Nux Vomica	311	Vulgaris Citrullus...	455
Symphytum officinale	142		
Symplocarpus fœtidus	86	Xanthium spinosum.	83
		" strumarium	127
Tanacetum vulgare..,	434	Xanthorhiza Apiifolia	469
Taraxacum Dens-leonis	159	Xanthoxylum Caro-	
Teucrium Canadensis	373	linianum	29
Thuja occidentalis	22	Xanthoxylum fraxineum	28
Thymus vulgaris	438		
Tilia Americana	42, 272	Zingiber officinalis..	202

CPSIA information can be obtained
at www.ICGtesting.com
Printed in the USA
BVHW041143220222
629783BV00007B/146